# CALMING SOCIAL ANXIETY FOR TEENS

# CALMING SOCIAL ANXIETY FOR TEENS

Simple CBT, ACT and Mindfulness practices to Boost Confidence, Overcome Fear, and Face Shyness in Groups

SARAH J. FOSTER

# Disclaimer Notice

The information and exercises in this book are intended for educational and informational purposes only. They are not a substitute for professional mental health diagnosis or treatment. If you are experiencing significant anxiety or any mental health condition, please consult with a licensed therapist or other qualified mental health professional.

The author and publisher strive to provide accurate and up-to-date information. However, the fields of psychology and mental health are constantly evolving. It is always best to seek personalized advice from a qualified professional regarding your specific needs and circumstances.

While the techniques in this book have the potential to be helpful, results are not guaranteed. The author and publisher are not responsible for any outcomes resulting from the use or misuse of the information provided. Your choices, actions, and results are your responsibility.

# Copyright Notice

**Kindread Publishing**

367 St Marks Ave Brooklyn,

NY 11238

https://www.kindread.org

**Calming Social Anxiety for Teens**



For more information, email info@kindread.org

**First Edition**

**ISBN: 9798891701236**

# PREFACE

I know how hard it is. The racing heart, the constant worry, the way even simple things can feel impossible. I know, because I've been there. Anxiety was my unwelcome companion for years. I wish I'd had a book like this – something to tell me I wasn't alone, that anxiety isn't a weakness, and that there were things I could do to fight back.

That's why I wrote this book. It won't erase your fears overnight, but it will give you a toolbox of proven techniques you can start using right now. We'll cover how your mind fuels anxiety, how to challenge those negative thoughts, and how some calming strategies can give you breathing room. It's about building confidence, one small step at a time.

You are stronger than your anxiety wants you to believe, and I'm here to help you prove it.

*Sarah J. Foster*

# CONTENTS

# TAKE CHARGE OF YOUR SOCIAL ANXIETY

# INSIDE THIS PART

Okay, if you're reading this, chances are things have gotten…tough. Maybe you feel on edge all the time, or completely freeze up in social situations. Feeling awkward is one thing, but when it starts getting in the way of making friends, doing well in school, or just having fun? That's when it's time to take a closer look.

See, I work with a lot of teens, and so many of you are awesome, smart, and hilarious, but get held back by anxiety. This book is about understanding what's really going on, and – more importantly – learning to change that. Think of me as your guide, helping you figure out the whole anxiety puzzle and build the skills to break free from it. But here's the thing: you don't have to let anxiety rule your life. This book is your toolkit for taking charge. We will break down exactly what's going on with those anxious thoughts and feelings and give you real strategies to cope. It might not always be easy, but I promise, you can learn to chill out more, feel way more confident, and start actually enjoying those things you've been avoiding. Let's do this!

# SOCIAL ANXIETY OR JUST TEEN LIFE? LET'S BREAK IT DOWN

Ever feel like those awkward moments control your life? Big tests, parties, even just chilling with friends – sometimes the nerves take over. But how do you know if it's normal jitters or that "hide under a rock" feeling? Feeling nervous from time to time is normal, but sometimes that anxiety goes into overdrive. If you recognize yourself in a lot of the following, it might be a sign you're dealing with social anxiety, not just the usual teen jitters:

- **Anxiety Attack!** Not just butterflies, but feeling on edge before almost every social thing.

- **Mind-Freeze & Body Meltdown**: Your mind goes blank, you start sweating, heart pounding – basically, panic mode.
- **Avoidance is King**: You skip stuff you want to do, just to dodge that fear. Friends, clubs, whatever – anxiety calls the shots.

But is that awkwardness just part of being a teen, or is there something more going on? Are you a bit shy, or possibly introverted? Or is it that panicky feeling that has a serious, negative impact on your life? Let's dig in and decode what's really happening. Here's the difference:

- **Shyness**: Feeling a bit nervous in some situations, but it doesn't stop you from doing what you want.
- **Introversion**: You actually enjoy some alone time, and big social stuff can be draining. But it's a choice, not a fear thing.
- **Social Anxiety**: That crushing panic that makes it feel impossible to be yourself around others.

Understanding what you're facing is the first step to feeling better. Social anxiety isn't a diagnosis to be scared of, it's a signal that you need better tools to manage those anxious feelings. Ready to bust a BIG anxiety myth? You can't just "snap out of it". Nope. Anxiety, especially social anxiety happens because your brain's alarm system is a bit overactive. This isn't about being weak or not trying. It's about learning to calm that alarm system and build new ways of thinking. (And don't worry, we'll get to how soon!)

Your brain and body are playing tricks on you, making you feel that way. The Anxiety Triangle reveals their secrets – and how to fight back!



✓ Emily: Parties? Nope. Presentations? Disaster! Even hanging with friends sometimes leads to canceling plans. Her mind races with worst-case scenarios, and her body freaks out. This is classic social anxiety.

✓ Michael: He's quiet in class, and prefers hanging with a few close friends. But honestly, he's okay with it. He might be shy, or a bit introverted, but he's not held back by fear.

✓ Anna: Big groups drain her energy, so she recharges with solo time. However, if she really wants to go to that concert, she'll push herself. That's introversion, not anxiety.

✓ Challenge: Where do your social worries fall on the scale? This is the first step to understanding your own unique brand of social anxiety. Don't worry if you feel in-between categories — that's totally normal! The goal is to get a clearer picture of how anxiety shows up for you.

✓ Instructions:
- Find your spot on the spectrum below. Remember, this can change as you learn new skills!
- Be honest! This is just for you, to get a sense of where you might fall on the spectrum.
- It's okay to be in between! You can place your mark anywhere on the line.

✓ Spectrum:
- Mild Shyness: "Butterflies before a party, but you still go and have fun"
- Moderate Shyness: "Sometimes hold back in groups, worry a bit about what people think"
- Occasional Social Anxiety: "Certain situations (presentations, etc.) feel really scary, but it's manageable most of the time"
- Frequent Social Anxiety: "Anxiety interferes with things you want to do, makes it hard to be yourself around others"
- Severe Social Anxiety: "Feeling panicked or trapped in most social situations, avoidance is a big problem"

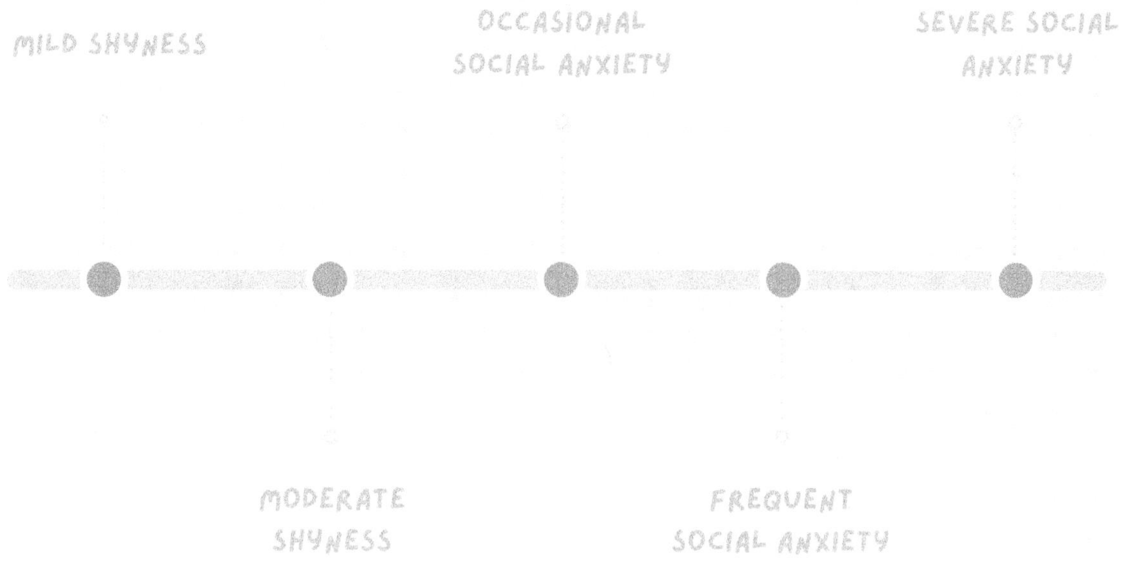


✓ Why This Matters:

- Self-Awareness is Key: Understanding the level of shyness or anxiety you experience is the first step towards choosing the right tools to manage it.
- Not a Label: This isn't about putting yourself in a box. It's about finding strategies that match your needs.
- Progress Tracking: We will revisit this exercise later to see how your experiences change as you learn new skills!

# THE ANXIETY TRIANGLE: HOW EVERYTHING CONNECTS

Okay, if you've ever felt trapped by anxiety, it's time to break free! Understanding the Anxiety Triangle isn't just about knowing why you feel the way you do, it's about unlocking how to change it. Think of it as the secret code to getting your power back.

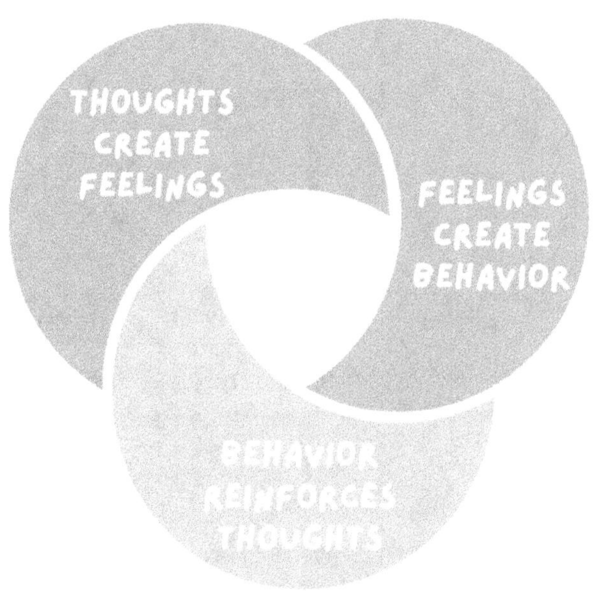


So, what the heck is the Anxiety Triangle anyway? It's basically a diagram showing how your thoughts, physical feelings, and behaviors all fuel each other, creating that crazy anxiety spiral. Let's break it down:

- **Thoughts:** Those racing worries about what people think, how you might mess up, basically everything that could go wrong.
- **Feelings:** Not just the nerves, but your body going into full-on panic mode – heart pounding, sweating, that shaky feeling.
- **Behaviors:** What you DO because of the thoughts and feelings – canceling plans, avoiding eye contact, staying quiet even when you want to speak up.

Why does this even matter? Because each part of the triangle makes the others WORSE. Negative thought? Your body freaks out. Body freaking out? Your mind races even more. And those avoidant behaviors? They might bring temporary relief, but long-term they trap you in the anxiety cycle.

But here's the good news (yes, really!): the Anxiety Triangle might feel like your enemy right now, but you can flip it! By learning to change any part of the triangle, the whole thing starts to weaken. Calmer thoughts? Your body chills out a bit. Facing a small fear? Your thoughts become less negative.

Get ready to take control! The rest of this book is about giving you tools to tackle each part of that triangle. It's not magic, but it IS powerful. You're about to become an expert at breaking that anxiety spiral and feeling way more in charge of your life.

✓ **Emily's Party Spiral:** Remember Emily? The one who dreads parties and worries about every little thing? Here's how her Anxiety Triangle typically works: A thought pops into her head: "Everyone will see how awkward I am. They're all going to judge me." Immediately, her heart starts pounding, her palms get sweaty, and she feels like she might throw up. Instead of facing the party, she makes a last-minute excuse and cancels on her friend. She stays home feeling relieved, but also deeply disappointed in herself. The next time a party comes around, even the IDEA of it fills her with dread. Now, she's not just anxious; she's also the "flaky friend," adding another layer to her worries.

✓ **The Presentation Panic:** Imagine you're in class, ready to present. For some teens, this feels like facing a firing squad! Here's a classic anxiety spiral: "I'll mess this up, forget what to say, and everyone will laugh." Their face flushes, voice shakes, and their mind goes blank. To get it over with, they rush through the slides, mumble, and avoid making eye contact. Next time a presentation comes up, just the thought triggers that familiar panicky feeling, making it even harder to focus.

## EXERCISE 2: FLIP THE SCRIPT

✓ Challenge: Ready to take control of those panicky thoughts? Negative self-talk has a way of hijacking your brain, especially in social situations. But the good news is, you can learn to fight back! Below, you'll practice "flipping the script" on those anxious thoughts. It might feel awkward at first, but the more you do it, the easier it gets to talk back to that inner critic.

✓ Instructions: Presentations can be seriously stressful! But remember, the Anxiety Triangle isn't all-powerful – you CAN fight back. Here's how to start flipping those negative thought spirals:

Step 1: The Trigger

Imagine giving a presentation. That first wave of panic hits with a familiar thought: "I'm going to mess this up. I'll forget what to say, and everyone will laugh."

Step 2: Flip the Script!

Take that negative thought, and reframe it in one of these ways:

- Realistic: "I might make some mistakes, but that's normal. Most people won't even notice."
- Neutral: "I've practiced this, and I'm prepared. I'll just focus on getting through it."
- Challenging: "Okay, what if I DO stumble? It won't be the end of the world."

✓ Keep practicing! The more you flip those negative scripts, the weaker their power gets. Think of other stressful social situations. Jot down those automatic thoughts, then challenge them! It might feel awkward at first, but it gets easier, we promise!

| Thought Trap | Reality Check |
| --- | --- |
|  |  |
|  |  |
|  |  |
|  |  |
|  |  |

# ARE YOU SOCIALLY ANXIOUS OR JUST SHY? (THE QUIZ!)

Sometimes it's easier to understand how social anxiety feels from within. Take a look at these two examples – see if any of this sounds familiar:

## IN ACTION: MISSED OPPORTUNITIES

✓ **Emily's Dread:** Remember Emily? The one who cancels on friends at the last minute? It's not that she doesn't WANT to go to the party. Days beforehand, her mind is racing. She pictures herself standing alone, everyone whispering about her awkward outfit, or saying the wrong thing. The anxiety gnaws at her until staying home feels like the only way to make it stop.

✓ **The Classroom Freeze:** Imagine you're sitting in class, and the teacher asks a question. You know the answer, but your heart starts pounding just thinking about raising your hand. What if your voice cracks? What if you say something dumb? So, you stay silent. Afterwards, you feel annoyed at yourself, wishing you could have just gone for it.

Did Emily's dread, or that feeling of freezing when you want to speak up, hit a little too close to home? It's okay! Recognizing these patterns is the first step towards breaking them. And that's where this quiz comes in — it's about getting clearer on whether it's full-on social anxiety or shyness holding you back. Either way, this book is packed with tools to help you feel more confident and less trapped by those fears.

## EXERCISE 3: THE QUIZ

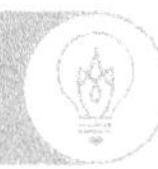

✓  Instructions:

- No overthinking! Answer honestly about how you feel MOST of the time.
- Circle YES or NO for each question.
- At the end, we'll break down what your answers might mean.

✓  Let's Get Started:

1. Do you dread events with people you don't know well, even casual stuff? YES NO
2. Before social situations, do you imagine everything going horribly wrong? YES NO
3. Does your body go haywire (sweating, shaky, etc.) in social situations? YES NO

4. Do you find yourself getting super irritable or having angry outbursts before having to go out or be social? YES NO

5. Do you constantly compare yourself to everyone else, feeling like you fall short? YES NO

6. Do you avoid stuff you'd LIKE to do, just to avoid the anxiety? YES NO

7. Is it hard to speak in class, even if you know the answer? YES NO

8. Does the fear of being judged sometimes overwhelm? YES NO

9. Do you worry for days or weeks beforehand about upcoming social events? YES NO

10. Do you replay awkward moments in your head for way too long? YES NO

✓ What It Means:

- Mostly YES Answers: Social anxiety might be what you're dealing with. It's more intense than shyness, but this book has your back!

- Mostly NO Answers: You might be on the shy side, which is okay! If a few "yes" answers felt true, you'll still find helpful tools in this book.

- A Mix of Answers: This is common! You might be shy, with some moments where anxiety is stronger.

Okay, now that you've taken the quiz, you might have some new thoughts about where your anxiety falls. Let's revisit that spectrum and see if anything has shifted for you:

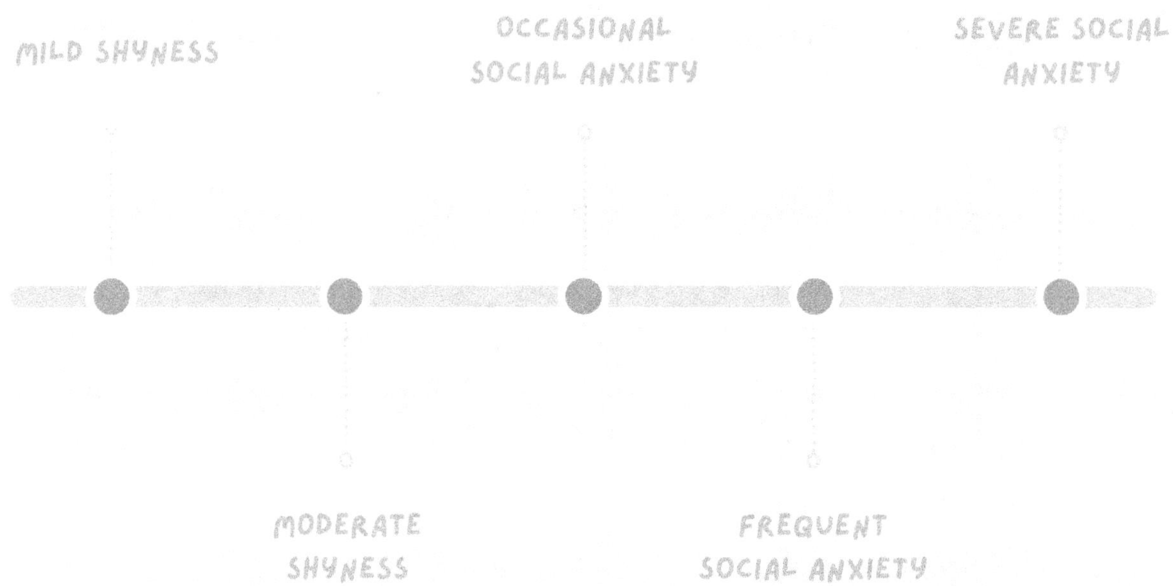


✓ Instructions:

- Take a moment to reflect: Do your quiz results change how you see yourself on this spectrum?
- Place a new mark: Put an 'X' where you think you fall now. It's okay if it's in a similar spot, or totally different!
- Notice, Don't Judge: The goal isn't to "improve" your score, but to get a clearer picture of your own experience.

# WHY SOCIAL ANXIETY SUCKS (AND HOW THIS BOOK MAKES IT SUCK WAYYY LESS)

Social anxiety has a knack for making simple things feel impossible. It warps your perspective, throws up roadblocks, and makes you question yourself at every turn. If any of these experiences resonate with you, know that you're not alone:

- **The Missed Connections**: You long to connect with others, to join in on the fun, but fear gets in the way, leaving you feeling isolated and stuck.

- **Mind Games:** Your own mind seems to work against you, conjuring up worst-case scenarios and magnifying every potential misstep. It's a relentless battle to quiet those negative thoughts.

- **Energy Drain**: Social interactions, even seemingly small ones, can be surprisingly draining. A simple conversation can leave you feeling as exhausted as if you'd just finished a workout.
- **The "What Ifs"**: It's easy to get trapped in a loop of overthinking, replaying awkward moments, and agonizing over what you could have done differently. You wish you could turn back time and have a do-over.
- **Feeling Like an Alien**: It can feel like everyone else has this social stuff down pat while you're struggling to keep up. This can make you feel alone and misunderstood, but remember, tons of people struggle with this – you're not weird or broken.

You know that feeling, right? That desire to jump into the conversation, to go to that party, to raise your hand in class...but there's something holding you back. It's like there's an invisible wall between you and those experiences you crave. That's social anxiety. It makes you feel frustrated, left out like you're missing out on something important. And you're right, it's a major bummer. But here's the thing: understanding social anxiety and having the right tools to face it is where the game changes.

Think of this book as your own decoder ring for social anxiety. We're going to take it apart, figure out how it works, and why your brain sometimes throws these curveballs. Sometimes, it's just normal teen awkwardness, but sometimes it's more than that. Knowing what you're dealing with is like getting the cheat codes for a tough level. Speaking of tough levels, those negative thoughts in your head can feel like the final boss of social situations. They whisper that you're going to fail, that everyone is judging you – your own brain becomes your worst enemy! We're not having that. It's time for a serious mindset upgrade. We'll learn how to challenge those sneaky thoughts, calm that panicky inner critic, and get some science-backed tricks to change your tune.

Now, here's the deal: overcoming social anxiety is a journey, not a sprint. We're going to break things down into steps. Think of it like leveling up in your favorite game – you wouldn't start by facing the final boss, would you? You'll build your social stamina gradually. Each challenge you face, even the small ones, makes you a little stronger.

This book isn't about turning you into some fake super-extrovert. It's about giving you the skills and confidence to manage social stuff your way and on your terms. Imagine reading the last chapter and feeling less afraid to try new things, to speak up, and to connect with people without that constant feeling of dread. That's the power of the tools we're about to learn. The strategies in this book are like power-ups for your brain.

Okay, we've covered just how much those social worries can hold you back. But here's the deal: understanding how your brain works is the first step towards getting a handle on this. Let's dive into how CBT and mindfulness can change the game.

## EXERCISE 4: THE "WHAT IF" FLIP 

✓ **Challenge:** Ready to turn those worries around? It's time to fight back against those "what if..." thoughts that hijack your brain. Let's try flipping them into possibilities that are less scary, and maybe even a little exciting!

✓ **Instructions:**

- Write down 3-5 negative "What if..." thoughts that pop into your head before social events.
- Next to each one, rewrite it into a more positive or neutral "What if..."

✓ **Examples:**

- "What if I say something stupid?" -> "What if I contribute something interesting to the conversation?"
- "What if I trip and fall in front of everyone?" -> "What if no one even notices?"
- "What if they don't like me?" -> "What if I meet people I have something in common with?"

## The Worry Whirlpool

## The "What If" Reframe

# THIS ISN'T MAGIC: HOW CBT AND MINDFULNESS ACTUALLY WORK

Okay, let's cut to the chase. You probably already know there's no magic potion to erase social anxiety overnight. I mean, if there was, wouldn't everyone be using it? But while there's no sparkly fix-all solution, tools like CBT and mindfulness can be total game-changers. Think of them less like spells and more like superpowers you learn to unlock.

**So, what's CBT all about?** Short for Cognitive Behavioral Therapy, it sounds complicated, but it's actually pretty straightforward. CBT is like detective work for your brain. You know how social anxiety can plant those negative thoughts that make things seem way worse than they are? CBT is about catching those sneaky thoughts and challenging them. It's about replacing exaggerated worries ("This is going to be a disaster!") with more realistic thinking.

Picture this: It's the night before a big presentation, and your brain goes into overdrive. "You're going to bomb," it whispers. "Everyone will laugh, and you'll wish you could vanish into thin air." That's social anxiety doing its thing, and CBT helps you fight back. Together, we'll learn to track down those sabotaging thoughts and challenge them. Is it REALLY guaranteed that everyone will think you're an idiot? Or is your brain just playing an epic horror movie in your head? It's time for a reality check to replace those catastrophic predictions with something more balanced and less terrifying. It's your brain, and you get to call the shots.

Now, what's the deal with mindfulness? Think of mindfulness as a superpower "pause" button for those intense moments of anxiety. It's about getting out of your head and focusing on the present – how your body feels, and what's happening around you. That helps calm your racing mind and brings you back to reality. Mindfulness is also about noticing those pesky thoughts and feelings that pop up without getting swept up in them. Imagine them as clouds passing by in the sky – they might be dark and stormy, but they aren't permanent. Mindfulness helps you even deal with that super-critical voice you hear sometimes, the one telling you you're not good enough. We'll practice ditching that harsh judgment and replacing it with a dose of self-compassion.

CBT and mindfulness are a dynamic duo. CBT changes how you think, and mindfulness gives you tools to cope with those overwhelming feelings that come with social anxiety. It's not about feeling amazing all the time – because hey, life isn't all sunshine and rainbows. But it is about facing difficult social situations with more power and less panic. This stuff takes work. You'll stumble sometimes, and that's perfectly okay. But with every challenge you face, you'll prove to yourself that you're way stronger than you think.

Let's be real: mastering your social anxiety won't happen overnight. There will be difficult days and moments when you want to give up. That's totally normal! But the awesome part is, that with every challenge you face, you build resilience. Let's get ready to face those tough moments head-on.

## IN ACTION: MICHAEL'S TURNAROUND

Michael used to dread group projects. Speaking up triggered a storm of self-doubt: "They'll think I'm stupid," and "I'm going to mess up." He'd hide in the back, hoping to stay invisible. But learning CBT and mindfulness changed everything. At first, just noticing those racing thoughts made Michael even more anxious. Slowly, he chipped away at those negative beliefs ("Everyone's judging me" wasn't always true), replacing them with kinder ones. Mindfulness taught him to watch the wave of anxiety rise and fall... without getting swept away. The next group project was still nerve-wracking. But instead of giving in, Michael set a small goal: speak up once each meeting. The first time was shaky, but he DID IT. Afterwards, he focused on that victory, not the stumbles. Michael still gets anxious sometimes, but now he has the tools. It's about progress, not perfection — and taking those brave steps forward anyway.

# THE REAL DEAL: SERIOUSLY, WHY SO HARD?

Okay, let's not sugarcoat it: working on social anxiety is no walk in the park. Some days it'll feel awesome when you use a new technique and it actually helps. But there will also be times when you want to scream into a pillow, throw the book at a wall, and swear you'll never leave your room again. And that's totally normal.

Think of it like starting a new sport or learning a complicated video game. You're not going to be a pro overnight. There will be times you fumble, maybe even look a little silly trying a new skill. But you do it anyway because you're determined to get better. Beating social anxiety is kinda like that.

You'll face setbacks. Maybe that presentation still makes you super nervous even after practicing those thought-challenging techniques we learned. Or you try going to that party, but end up leaving way earlier than you hoped. It's tempting to see those moments as failures, to let your inner critic take over with the whole "See, I knew you couldn't do it" speech.

But here's the thing: it's not about being perfect. It's about progress. Did you try challenging those negative thoughts before the presentation, even if you still felt a bit shaky? Did you show up to the party in the first place, even if you didn't stay as long as you wanted? Those are wins! Every time you challenge yourself, every time you face down that fear instead of running away, you become a little stronger.

Some days will be harder than others. That's okay. Allow yourself to feel the frustration, the disappointment, without letting those feelings define you. Bad days don't erase all the progress you've made. This journey has ups and downs, but the general direction is forward.

And remember, you're not alone in this. I'm here, this book is here, and there are tons of other teens who get it. We'll figure this out – one challenge, one skill, one small victory at a time. Facing social anxiety head-on takes serious guts. The awesome part is that the tools you're about to learn will make it easier with each step. Let's ditch the overwhelm and start building your social anxiety-fighting toolkit.

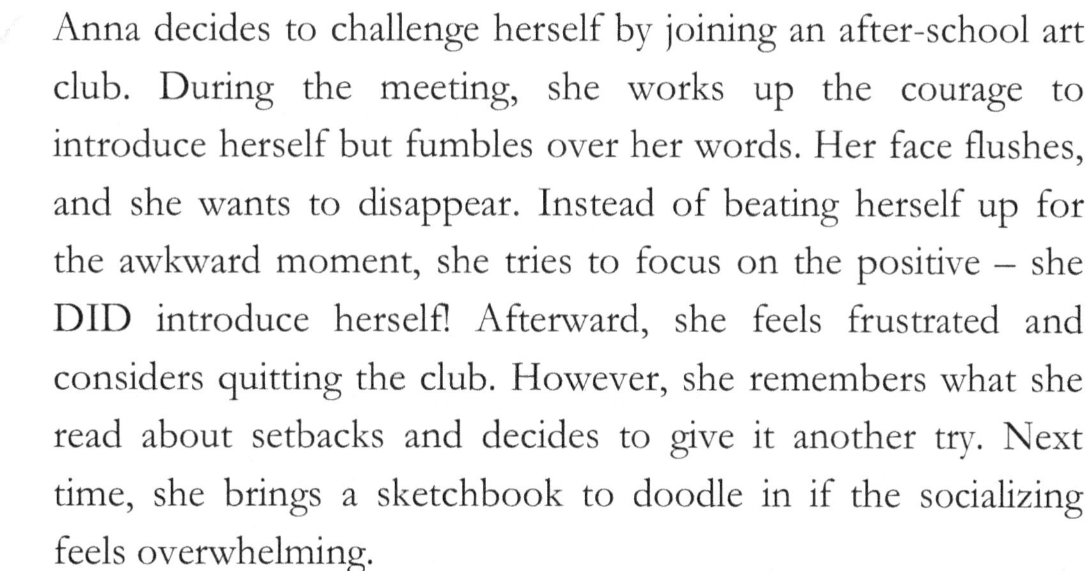


Anna decides to challenge herself by joining an after-school art club. During the meeting, she works up the courage to introduce herself but fumbles over her words. Her face flushes, and she wants to disappear. Instead of beating herself up for the awkward moment, she tries to focus on the positive – she DID introduce herself! Afterward, she feels frustrated and considers quitting the club. However, she remembers what she read about setbacks and decides to give it another try. Next time, she brings a sketchbook to doodle in if the socializing feels overwhelming.

## EXERCISE 5: THE BAD DAY PLAN 

✓ **Challenge:** Let's face it, working on social anxiety means some days are going to be extra tough. Frustration, disappointment, and the urge to hide from the world are completely normal. Having a plan for those bad days makes them a little less overwhelming. Below write down your top 3 soothing activities. Keep the list handy on your phone or someplace you'll see it. This isn't about making your anxiety magically disappear. It's about having tools to ride out the rough moments, to remind yourself that bad days don't last forever.

✓ **What soothes you?** Think of 3-5 go-to activities that help you chill out, de-stress, or just distract yourself in a healthy way. This could include:
  - **Music:** A mood-boosting playlist, calming songs, or playing an instrument.
  - **Movement:** Taking a walk, dancing around your room, a short workout video.
  - **Sensory Stuff:** A cozy blanket, hot bath, playing with a fidget toy, smelling something calming (like lavender).
  - **Connection:** Talking to a friend, family member, or pet.
  - **Creativity:** Drawing, journaling, building something - whatever gets you absorbed.

Part 1:

# TAMING YOUR SOCIAL ANXIETY MACHINE

# INSIDE THIS PART

Get ready to outsmart your social anxiety! In this section, we're going undercover to expose how it tries to control you. We'll bust those negative thoughts that make everything seem way worse than it is, figure out why your body freaks out, and pinpoint exactly what sends you into a worry spiral. This isn't about feeling bad – it's about getting the tools to take charge.

Think of your social anxiety as a glitchy app making your life way harder. Time to update your system! We're going to rewire those panicky thoughts, learn how to chill out when your body's in fight-or-flight mode, and face those scary situations step-by-step. It might not always be easy, but every challenge you tackle makes you stronger. Get ready to ditch the fear and start feeling way more unstoppable!

# CHAPTER 1:
# THOUGHT POLICE: BUSTING THOSE BS BELIEFS

Ever notice how your brain turns into a total drama queen with social anxiety? It tells you everyone's judging you, that you're about to embarrass yourself, etc. Ugh, who needs that negativity? Time to put those unhelpful thoughts on trial! In this chapter, we're learning how to identify those thinking errors, cross-examine them with logic, and start talking back like the boss you are.

## THOUGHT TRAPS EXPOSED! (UNMASKING THINKING ERRORS)

Okay, picture this: You're about to walk into that party, give a class presentation, try out for the team... whatever situation makes your social anxiety go haywire. Your brain starts blasting a horror movie soundtrack in your head: "Everyone will think you're weird... you're going to say something totally stupid... this is gonna be a disaster!"

Those thoughts are like those super annoying pop-up ads that take over your screen – totally distracting you from what matters, and they're usually totally WRONG. That's why the first step in busting social anxiety is becoming a Thought Detective.

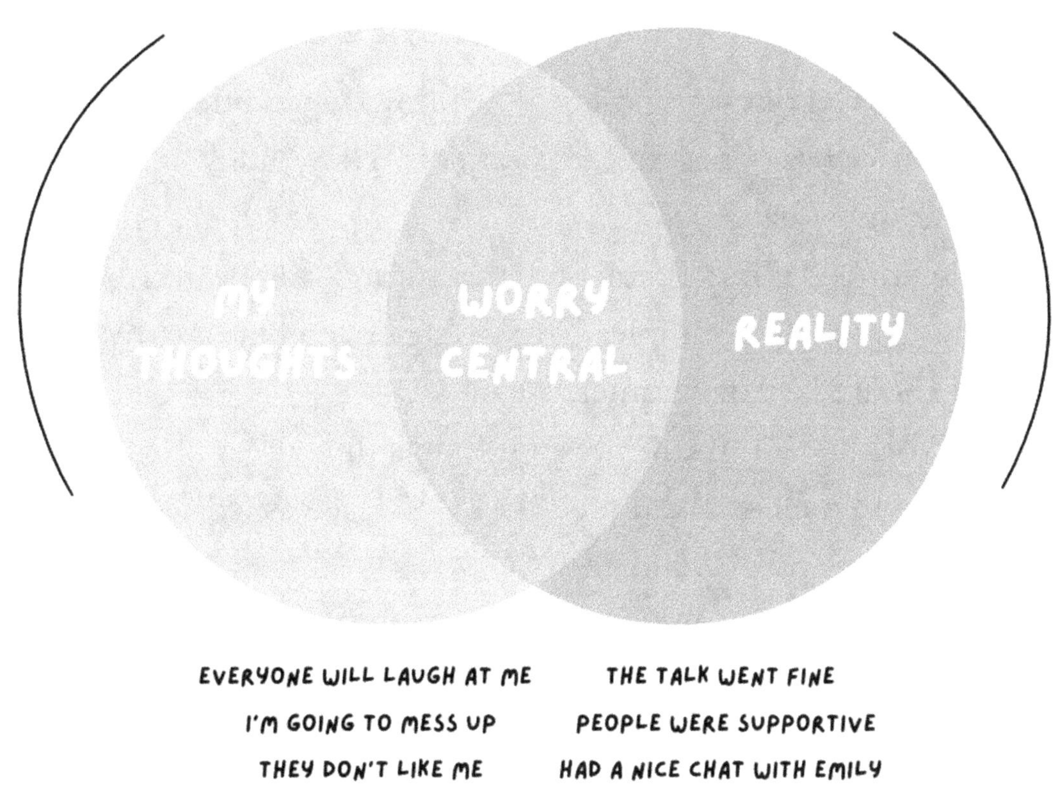


Imagine your brain as a little overprotective bodyguard, the kind who searches your backpack for danger before letting you go to the mall! Social anxiety loves to team up with that bodyguard, whispering all sorts of nonsense in your ear to convince you that a situation is way scarier than it actually is. That's where those sneaky "thought traps" come in. CBT teaches you to spot those "thought traps" – the times your brain is totally exaggerating or straight-up lying to you. Here are a few of the most common culprits:

- **The Catastrophizer**: Turning a minor setback into a major disaster. Predicting the absolute worst-case scenario will happen. Example: "I forgot one line in my presentation, and now everyone thinks I'm an idiot."
- **The Mind Reader**: Assuming you know what others are thinking and that it's always negative. Example: "They didn't text back right away, they must hate me."
- **The Fortune Teller**: Predicting the future will be terrible without any real evidence. Example: "I'm going to embarrass myself at the party, I should just stay home."
- **All-or-Nothing Thinking:** Seeing things in black-and-white with no room for gray areas. Example: "If I don't get asked to the dance, it proves no one will ever like me."
- **Filtering:** Focusing only on the negatives and ignoring anything positive. Example: "One person laughed during my presentation, so it was obviously a complete failure."

These traps are kind of like those spam emails promising you've won a million dollars – tempting to believe for a second, but totally bogus! That's why your first line of defense is spotting those traps when they pop up. Once you can name the trick your brain is playing ("Okay, that's classic catastrophizing right there..."), it makes it a lot easier to challenge them and choose a more realistic thought.

Now that you know how your brain tries to trick you, are you ready to answer back? Get ready for some serious thought-challenging skills!"

## PARENT TIP: SPOTTING THOUGHT TRAPS

✓ Tune Into Their Talk: Listen for those all-or-nothing statements ("Nobody will ever like me", "I'm going to fail this test"). Don't rush to argue – just reflect back on what you're hearing, "Wow, that sounds really stressful." This opens the door for them to tell you more.

✓ Gently Question the Drama Instead of, "That's not true", try: "Is there any other way to look at this?", or "What's the evidence for that thought?". This gets them thinking, not defensive.

✓ Celebrate Tiny Shifts: Notice when they adjust their own negativity ("Okay, maybe not everyone will hate me...") This reinforces their ability to manage those anxious thoughts.

# CHALLENGE AND CONQUER: TIME TO TALK BACK TO YOUR BRAIN

Remember those sneaky thought traps we talked about – the catastrophizing, the mind-reading, all those ways your brain convinces you things are way worse than they really are? Well, good news: you don't have to sit there and take it! It's time to upgrade your mental self-defense skills and start fighting back. Think of it like this: your brain is that annoying friend who's always putting you down. "You're gonna sound like an idiot... Everyone's secretly judging you..." They tell you the same stuff over and over until you start to believe it.

But here's the thing: that voice in your head? It's not your boss! CBT teaches you how to talk back to those negative thoughts like you would to a mean friend. You don't have to accept everything they (or your brain!) tell you.

How do you actually do that? Here are a few ways:

- **Ask for evidence:** "Okay, brain, you say everyone's gonna laugh at me. What makes you so sure?"
- **Play devil's advocate:** "What would a truly supportive friend say right now?"
- **Reality check:** "Has this actually happened before? Or am I fortune-telling?"

It might feel a little weird at first like you're arguing with yourself! But the more you practice challenging those negative thought traps, the weaker they become. This is how you train your brain to work WITH you, not against you.

Talking back to your brain takes practice, and that's okay! With every challenge, you're building those mental muscles and taking back control. Now, let's figure out why your brain gets so worked up... Understanding your body's stress signals is the next step to calming that chaos.

## IN ACTION: TALKING BACK TO THE WORRIES 

✓ **The Presentation Panic.** Before his big presentation, Michael's brain went into overdrive. He wasn't just nervous, he was convinced he'd blank out in front of the entire class, stammer like an idiot, and everyone would laugh. The night before, he couldn't sleep, replaying his worst-case scenario over and over. **Challenge:** Tired of feeling defeated, Michael decided to try something new. "Okay, brain," he said, "I know you're scared, but have you considered that all that practice might actually pay off? And guess what? Even if I stumble a bit, it's not the end of the world." Focusing on what was within his control (his preparation) and reminding himself that everyone makes mistakes sometimes helped him finally fall asleep.

✓ **The Party Invite.** Anna really wanted to ask someone new from her science class to hang out. They seemed cool, and she was tired of hangingg with the same friends. But the second she thought about it, her anxiety kicked in. "They're gonna theink I'm weird," she thought. It felt easier to just not even try. **Challenge:** Anna realized she was mind-reading again. "Stop," she told herself, "I can't know what they'll say unless I ask. Maybe they'd be excited I reached out!" Instead of focusing on the worst possible outcome, Anna decided to give it a shot.

## EXERCISE 6: THOUGHT TRAPS CHALLENGE 

✓ Challenge: Ready to bust those negative thought traps? This worksheet is your secret weapon! Here's how it works:

1. The Trigger: What's the situation that's got you feeling anxious? Be specific!
2. The Thought Bully: What's that negative thought your brain keeps throwing at you? Write it down exactly as it pops into your head.
3. Name the Trap: Which thought trap is at work? (Catastrophizing, mind-reading, etc.)

✓ Example:

- Situation: Giving a presentation in class
- Negative Thought: I'm going to forget everything and everyone will laugh at me.
- Thought Trap: Catastrophizing, Fortune-Telling

Situation:

1.

_______________________________________________

2.

_______________________________________________

3.

_______________________________________________

Negative Thought:

1.

2.

3.

Thought Trap:

1.

2.

3.

# CHAPTER 2:

# YOUR ANXIOUS BRAIN AND BODY: WHY THIS HAPPENS

Ever feel like social anxiety messes with your body just as much as your head? That heart pounding, sweating like crazy, feeling seriously out of control – it's the worst! Why does your body freak out like this, even when your logical brain knows it's not actually dangerous?

In this chapter, we're going under the hood to understand why social anxiety makes you feel like you're in the middle of a disaster zone. Think of your brain and body as having an outdated alarm system, sending out all the wrong signals when you're around people.

This isn't your fault! We're going to break down the science behind those panicky feelings and show you that these reactions are totally normal (even if they suck). Understanding is the first step to calming that chaos and feeling more in control.

# PANIC BUTTON 101: WHAT'S HAPPENING IN THERE?

WE'VE ALL BEEN THERE, RIGHT?

Okay, let's talk about those moments when your anxiety goes from a low hum to a full-blown panic attack. Your heart is pounding, you might feel dizzy, or like you need to run away and hide. What the heck is going on in your body?!

Here's the thing: You have an awesome built-in alarm system designed to protect you from danger. The problem is, that social anxiety sometimes tricks that system into thinking a party or a presentation is a life-or-death situation.

**Let's break it down:**

- **The Amygdala:** AKA Your Brain's Lookout Tower. This little part of your brain scans for threats. Back in caveman days, that meant spotting a hungry tiger. Nowadays? It might mistake giving a class presentation for facing a deadly predator.
- **Fight, Flight, or Freeze:** When your amygdala freaks out, it triggers a whole cascade of stress hormones in your body. This is what gets you ready to either fight the danger, run away super-fast, or freeze up completely. Totally helpful when you're in actual danger... not so much when you're just trying to order lunch in the cafeteria.
- **The Thinking Brain Takes a Backseat:** Here's the tricky part — when you're in full-on panic mode, the rational part of your brain kind of goes offline. That's why it's hard to talk yourself down logically.

The good news? Understanding this process is the first step in hacking your anxiety response. Just knowing that your body is having a false alarm (even if it feels super real) can help you start to calm that system down. Understanding that racing heart, and sweaty palms moments is a huge step, but anxiety isn't just about what's in your head. Your feelings play a big role too. Ready to decode those emotions and why they sometimes go haywire?

## EXERCISE 7: UNDERSTANDING YOUR AMYGDALA 

✓ **Challenge:** Your amygdala is like that overprotective lookout tower in your brain, scanning for threats to keep you safe. But sometimes it gets a little too trigger-happy, especially with social anxiety. It might seem silly, but putting words to your amygdala's crazy stories helps you see how out-of-proportion they are. This is the first step in separating those false alarms from reality so you can start calming your system down. Let's practice figuring out those false alarms:

**Step 1: Recall a Recent Panic.** Think of a specific time recently when you had a strong panic response. Maybe it was during a presentation, trying to make a new friend, or even just ordering food at a crowded restaurant.

**Step 2: What Did My Body Do?** Write down the physical sensations you felt: racing heart, shortness of breath, sweating, etc. Don't judge them, just notice what was happening.

**Step 3: The False Alarm Story.** Now, put yourself in your amygdala's shoes. What kind of LIFE-OR-DEATH situation might cause your body to react that way? Here are some examples:

- **Ordering lunch panic:** Amygdala story: "Everyone's watching me... I'm going to mess up my order and they'll think I'm an idiot... I need to escape!"
- **Presentation meltdown:** Amygdala story: "I'm forgetting everything... they'll know I'm a fake... they're judging my every move..."

**Step 4: Reality Check.** Okay, now take a deep breath and step back into your rational brain. What's the MOST LIKELY thing that would have happened in those situations? Would anyone have actually cared that much if you made a small mistake?

**Recent Panic:**

___________________________________________

___________________________________________

**What Did My Body Do?**

___________________________________________

___________________________________________

**False Alarm Story & Reality Check:**

___________________________________________

___________________________________________

# FEELING THE FEELS: UNDERSTANDING YOUR BODY'S ALARM SYSTEM

Remember that awesome (and sometimes super annoying) alarm system in your brain? Well, turns out, those physical panic symptoms – the pounding heart, feeling shaky, that urge to run and hide – aren't just random. They're your body's way of trying to help... even if that "help" is seriously misguided.

Consider how your emotions and your body are connected. When you're super excited, you might feel jumpy or get butterflies in your stomach. When you're embarrassed, your face might flush red. Anxiety is like those feelings turned up to MAX VOLUME.

**Here's how it works:**
- **Emotional Trigger:** Something sets off your social anxiety alarm (walking into a crowded room, a big presentation, etc.)
- **Your Body Misinterprets the Signal:** Instead of seeing "awkward social situation," your body often translates it as "DANGER! RED ALERT!"
- **Stress Hormones Surge:** Your body dumps adrenaline and other stress hormones into your system. These are meant to help you fight

or flee from actual danger... not give a class presentation.

- **Physical Symptoms Kick-In:** Racing heart, sweating, shortness of breath, dizziness – all designed to get you ready for action.

The thing is, those physical sensations can make you feel even MORE anxious, creating a vicious cycle. Feeling shaky just confirms that something must be terribly wrong, which makes your body freak out even harder... It's exhausting!

But here's the good news: Understanding this connection is the first step in calming your body. Noticing what you're feeling can help you separate those intense emotions from the (often exaggerated) stories your brain is telling you.

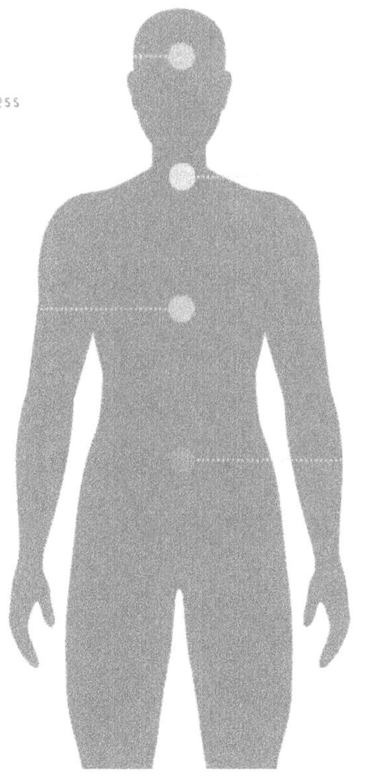

Important Note: Everyone experiences anxiety differently, and not all of these symptoms will apply to every person or every anxiety attack.

✓ **The Lunchroom Mishap.** Michael wasn't clumsy by nature, but with his secret crush sitting nearby, suddenly his hands turned into giant, awkward flippers. As his water glass toppled in slow motion, all he could think was, "This is it. I'm officially the biggest loser in school." His face burned, his heart pounded so hard he was sure the whole cafeteria could hear it, and time seemed to freeze as he waited for the laughter to erupt.

✓ **Stage Fright Strikes.** Emily knew her presentation inside and out. She'd practiced in the mirror a million times. But the moment she stood up in front of the class, it was like her brain short-circuited. A wave of nausea washed over her, her voice came out as a shaky squeak, and her mind went totally blank. The words she knew so well seemed to evaporate. All she could see were faces — some curious, maybe even a few pitying smirks. She wasn't sure if she was going to faint or throw up, but all she wanted was to disappear.

- ✓ **Focus on the Fight-or-Flight System:** Explain how anxiety is a normal biological response, like a built-in alarm system. Our brains are wired to keep us safe, and sometimes they go on high alert even when there's no real danger.

- ✓ **Validate Their Feelings:** Let them know this doesn't mean they're weak or crazy. Everyone's alarm system works a little differently.

- ✓ **Empowerment Through Knowledge:** Understanding the "why" behind anxiety can be calming. Knowing it's a response they can learn to manage is empowering.

# COMMON TRIGGERS: WHAT SETS OFF YOUR SOCIAL ANXIETY

Think of your social anxiety like a car alarm with a faulty sensor. Sometimes it goes off for legitimate reasons (like if someone's trying to break in). But most of the time, it starts blaring because a bird flew past the window, or the wind shook the car a little. It reacts to harmless things

What trips those wires? That's different for everyone, but here's the thing: identifying your biggest triggers is the key to disarming that anxiety alarm. Let's break down some of the most common culprits:

- **The Spotlight Effect:** You walk into a party and feel like all eyes are glued to you, judging your every move. Even when logically you know most people are too busy socializing to care what you're wearing, it can trigger major anxiety.
- **Performance Pressure:** Presentations, trying out for a team, even just getting called on in class... any situation where you feel like you're being evaluated can set off that alarm, even if you're totally prepared!
- **Fear of the Unknown:** New social situations, unfamiliar places, meeting new people – uncertainty is a huge trigger for a lot of teens with social anxiety. Your brain craves routine, and change can feel scary.
- **Awkwardness Alert:** Feeling like you don't know what to say, spilling your drink, or just those moments of uncomfortable silence... That fear of awkwardness can kick your anxiety into overdrive.
- **The Harsh Inner Critic:** Sometimes the biggest trigger isn't external, it's that mean voice in your head telling you you're going to mess up, that people secretly dislike you, and those other awful things.

This is just a start – your list of triggers might look totally different! The important thing is to notice the patterns. What situations, thoughts, or even certain people tend to set off that alarm? Once you uncover those, you can start developing strategies to outsmart them.

Knowing your triggers is like unlocking a level in a video game. You've figured out the enemy's weaknesses, now it's time to design a strategy to defeat them!

## EXERCISE 8: TRIGGER TRACKER

✓ **Challenge:** It might feel like your anxiety pops up at random, but there are usually patterns hiding beneath the surface. This tracker will help you decode those triggers so you can start taking control!

✓ **Instructions:**

- Whenever you feel a surge of anxiety, jot down the details in this chart below.
- Don't overthink it – just write down what comes to mind.
- On weekends, look for patterns. (Example: Do you always get anxious before gym class? Is there a certain thought that keeps popping up?)

✓ **Tips:**

- **Start Small:** Trying to track every anxiety pang is overwhelming. Aim for a few times per day.
- **No Judgments:** This is about getting curious, not beating yourself up!

Situation (Where were you? What were you doing?)

Physical Reaction (Heart racing, sweating, etc.)

Emotion (Scared, overwhelmed, etc.)

Thought (What was going through your head?)

# CHAPTER 3:

# THE FEAR ZONE: FACING YOUR WORST NIGHTMARES (STEP-BY-STEP)

Social anxiety loves to throw those "worst-case scenario" nightmares at you. You know, the ones about saying something stupid, everyone laughing, and you wanting to disappear. It feels impossible to even think about those situations without freaking out. But guess what? It's time to stop letting those fears control you.

Think of this chapter as your battle plan for facing those scary scenarios. It will not be easy, but we'll start small and build a "Bravery Ladder." You'll learn how to gradually expose yourself to the things you fear, proving to yourself you can handle it.

Promise: those terrifying moments will start to feel less overwhelming. You'll learn to manage those panicky feelings instead of running from them. Get ready to punch fear in the face and reclaim your power!

# LEVEL UP: BUILDING YOUR BRAVERY LADDER

Think of overcoming social anxiety like training for a major competition. You wouldn't expect to run a marathon without building up your stamina first, right? The same goes for building your bravery muscle! That's where the Bravery Ladder comes in.

Picture your biggest social fears stacked like rungs of a ladder. Maybe giving a presentation is way up at the top, while simply saying "hi" to someone new is closer to the bottom. The goal isn't to hurl yourself towards the highest rung – that's a recipe for panic. Instead, we're going to start with smaller challenges and gradually work our way upwards.

This approach works for a few reasons. First, each time you face something that makes you a little anxious and come out the other side, you're sending a powerful message to your brain: "Hey, I can handle this!" Those small victories build confidence over time. Secondly, exposure – purposely facing those scary situations – might feel awful at first, but it's the key to making them less intimidating. The more often you do something, the less your anxiety alarm freaks out about it. And most importantly, with a bravery ladder, you're in the driver's seat. Facing fears on your own terms is incredibly empowering.

## SAMPLE BRAVERY LADDER: SPEAKING UP IN CLASS

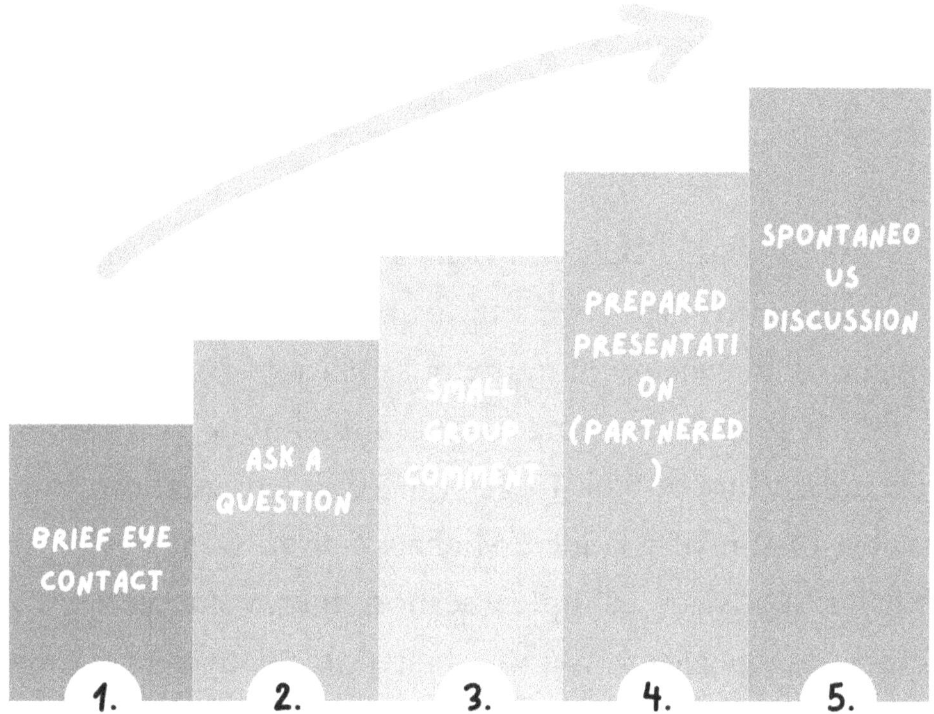


So, how do you build your ladder?

- **List Your Fears:** Brainstorm every social situation that makes your stomach churn, from the mildly stressful to the truly terrifying.
- **Rank Them:** Start with easier challenges at the bottom and the hardest ones at the top. Be super specific about what scares you (is it making eye contact, the fear of judgment, etc.?)
- **Start Climbing:** Once you've got your ladder, it's time to tackle that bottom rung! We'll talk about strategies for facing those challenges next.

Progress isn't always a straight line. Some challenges might take longer to overcome, and that's totally okay. The point is, with each step up that ladder, you're becoming a braver, more confident version of yourself!

## IN ACTION: SMALL STEPS, BIG WINS

✓ **The Shy Speaker.** Before, Michael would do anything to avoid speaking up in class, even if he knew the answer cold. The thought of all eyes on him, the possibility of stumbling over his words... it made his stomach twist into knots. Sometimes he'd even pretend to be sick to get out of a presentation. But after building his bravery ladder, Michael started small – first raising his hand to answer a simple question, then volunteering to read a short passage aloud. With each step, his confidence grew, and now he can even present in front of the class without feeling like he's going to faint.

✓ **From Wallflower to Social Butterfly (Kinda).** Emily used to dread parties. The noise, the crowds, the pressure to make conversation – it all felt incredibly overwhelming. She'd stand awkwardly on the sidelines, hoping to become invisible. But Emily was tired of missing out. Her bravery ladder started with the simple goal of smiling and making eye contact with a few people. Next, she challenged herself to strike up short conversations. Now, she's still not the life of the party, but she doesn't feel that crushing anxiety anymore, and she's even made a few new friends in the process.

## EXERCISE 9: ONE STEP AT A TIME

✓ **Challenge:** Facing a huge fear – like giving a presentation, joining a club, or going to a party – can feel completely overwhelming. That's where the power of your bravery ladder comes in! Let's break down a big challenge into smaller, more manageable steps.

✓ **Instructions:**
- **Choose Your Challenge:** Pick a social situation that fills you with major anxiety.
- **What Are the Scary Parts?:** Get specific about what makes you nervous.
- **Design Your Ladder:** Start with a bottom-rung challenge that feels slightly uncomfortable, but doable. Then, gradually work your way up to your ultimate fear.

✓ **Tips:**
- **Celebrate Small Wins:** Overcoming each rung is a huge

achievement!

- **It's Okay to Repeat a Rung:** If a certain step feels too hard, practice it more before moving up.

# EXPOSURE MISSIONS: IT GETS EASIER, WE PROMISE

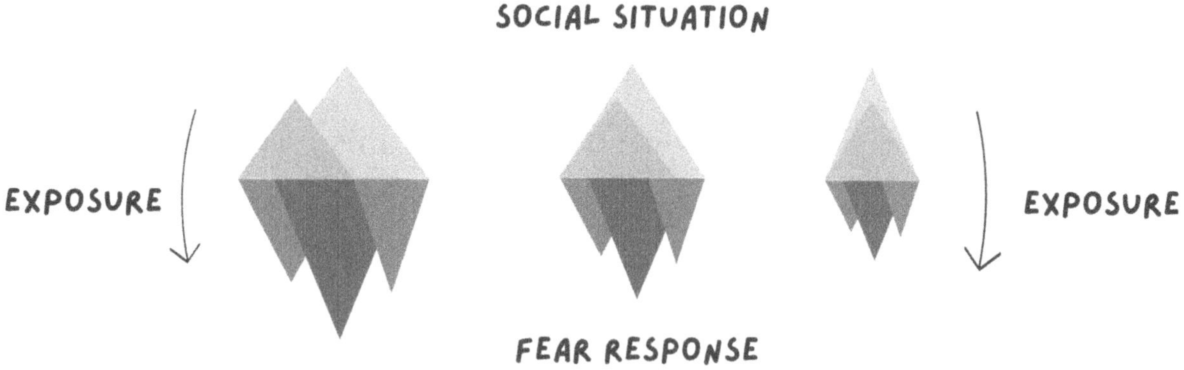


Think of those challenges on your bravery ladder. We've spent time building it, now it's time to start climbing! This is where we go from just surviving social anxiety to actually outsmarting it. Get ready for exposure missions.

Okay, I know what you're thinking: purposely making myself anxious sounds like the worst idea ever. But trust me, there's a method to this madness! Exposure means facing those uncomfortable situations head-on. It's like jumping into the pool when the water feels freezing – it sucks for a minute, but then your body adjusts.

When you face a fear, that familiar panic kicks in: the racing heart, the sweaty palms, the urge to run and hide. This is your brain's alarm system going into overdrive, trying to keep you "safe." The problem is, it's misinterpreting awkward conversations as actual threats. But here's the good news: that uncomfortable feeling is temporary. If you stick it out, your body naturally calms down, sending a signal to your brain: "Hey, we survived! Maybe this isn't as dangerous as I thought."

Think of exposure as leveling up your bravery. Imagine trying to beat a super-tough video game without building your skills first – impossible! Facing social anxiety is similar. The more exposure missions you complete, the less power those scary situations have over you.

The key is to start small. Trying to tackle your biggest fear right away is like facing the final boss on level one. Instead, use your bravery ladder! Begin with those bottom-rung challenges, gradually working your way up as you build confidence.

It might seem counterintuitive to purposely make yourself uncomfortable, but each time you do, you're not just coping – you're changing the way your brain reacts. You're proving that joining a conversation, giving a presentation, or whatever your fear might be, isn't as terrifying as you once thought. That's how you break free from social anxiety!

Remember, exposure isn't about jumping headfirst into your greatest fears. It's about gradual challenges that build confidence. Here are some starter missions based on common teen social anxieties:

- **Fear of Speaking Up:**
  - **Bottom Rung:** Raise your hand once in class, even if it's just to ask a simple question.
  - **Next Step:** Contribute a comment to a group discussion.
  - **Keep Climbing:** Volunteer to read a short passage aloud.
- **Small Talk Struggles:**
  - **Bottom Rung:** Make eye contact and smile at three people you don't know.
  - **Next Step:** Compliment someone ("Cool sneakers!").
  - **Keep Climbing:** Ask someone a question to start a conversation ("Do you know what the homework is?")
- **Party Panic:**
  - **Bottom Rung:** Go to a small gathering with one friend you trust.
  - **Next Step:** Try to talk to one new person at the party.
  - **Keep Climbing:** Attend a larger event and aim to chat with a few people.

Exposure can sometimes feel overwhelming, and that's okay! But what if you had ways to manage those intense feelings in the moment? Mindfulness is about giving you that control. Get ready to chill out – even while facing your biggest fears.

## PARENT TIP: EASIER EXPOSURE MISSIONS 

✓ **Start Super Small:** Suggest breaking down a scary task into mini-steps they feel less overwhelmed by. Ordering their own coffee, saying hi to one new person, etc.

✓ **Focus on Effort, Not Outcome:** Whether the outcome is perfect or awkward, praise their bravery for trying. This emphasizes that facing fears is the real win.

✓ **Be a Chill Cheerleader:** Your own anxiety can rub off on them. Try calm encouragement instead of being overly hyped ("You've got this, no matter what!")

Part 2:

# MINDFULNESS: YOUR SECRET SUPERPOWER

# INSIDE THIS PART

Think your mind is a runaway train of worry? Welcome to the club! Between social anxiety, school drama, and those random panic attacks, sometimes it feels impossible to shut off the noise. But here's the deal: mindfulness is like a secret remote control for your brain. In this section, you'll learn how to quiet that "monkey mind," focus on what's happening right now, and handle those anxious thoughts without letting them take over.

Forget those images of meditating monks – mindfulness is about tools you can use in the middle of a meltdown. We'll cover easy breathing techniques, how to break free from those worry loops, and even how to replace that mean inner voice with some self-compassion. Think of this as your superpower training – get ready to level up your calm and tell anxiety to take a hike!

# CHAPTER 4:

# MONKEY MIND VS. ZEN MASTER: TRAINING YOUR FOCUS

Ever feel like your brain's a runaway train, packed with worries about the past, future freakouts, and random panic attacks? Ugh, that mental chaos is exhausting! Time to tame that "monkey mind" and master your focus.

Think of mindfulness as your secret weapon for chilling out that noisy brain. In this chapter, you'll get easy-to-follow tools to bring your attention back to the here and now. We'll cover simple breathing techniques, how to break free from those worry loops, and tricks to instantly ground yourself when things get crazy. Get ready to trade that mental chaos for some serious zen vibes!

## "JUST BREATHE" – BUT LIKE, HOW?

You've probably heard a million adults say, "Just breathe!" when you're feeling stressed or anxious. And yeah, it's kind of annoying because... how does that actually help? But here's the thing: they're not entirely wrong. Your breath is a surprisingly powerful tool for calming down that crazy alarm system in your brain and body.

Think about how you breathe when you're panicking. Usually, it's short, shallow, and from your chest. This signals to your brain: "EMERGENCY! DANGER!" But by switching things up with purposeful breathing, you can actually send the opposite message: "Hey, things are okay, we can chill."

There's no single "right" way to breathe for anxiety. It's about finding what works for you! Here are a few techniques to kickstart your breathing superpower:

- **Triangle Breathing:** Starting at the left bottom of the triangle (see the following page for a visual representation of Triangle Breathing). Trace your finger up the side while you take a deep breath in. Hold your breath for 3 seconds as you slide down the other side. Breathe out along the bottom of the triangle. Repeat it until you are calm.
- **Belly Breathing:** Put one hand on your belly, and one on your chest. Try to breathe so your belly hand rises, while your chest mostly stays still. It's all about deep, calming breaths.
- **The Sigh of Relief:** Purposely take a slow, deep breath in, then let it out in a big sigh. This mimics your body's natural way of releasing tension.

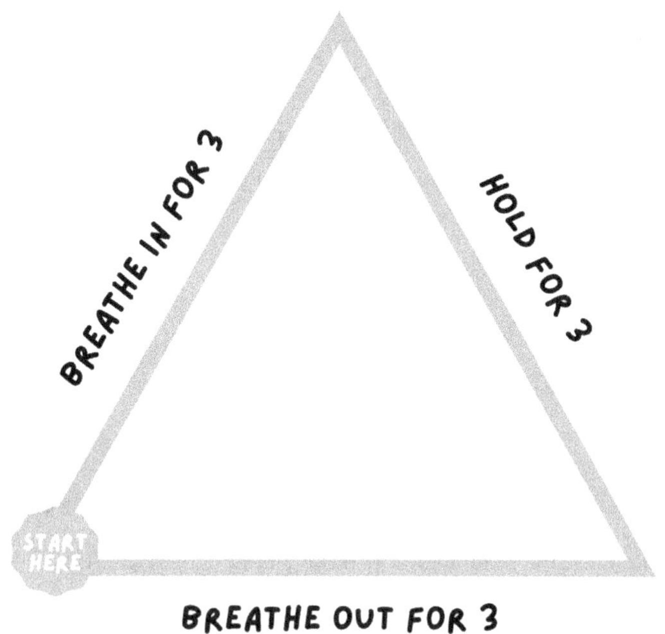


In the beginning, don't try these techniques in the middle of a full-blown panic attack – that's too overwhelming! Start by practicing for a few minutes each day when you're already somewhat calm. This builds your "breathing muscles". It might feel silly at first, but just like lifting weights gets easier with practice, so does mindful breathing.

Once you're comfortable with those techniques, they become your secret weapon during those exposure missions or when you feel that anxious wave rising. Don't expect perfection. The goal is to bring your anxiety down a few notches, not achieve total zen. This stuff takes practice, so don't get down on yourself if it feels awkward at first. The more you use your breath as a tool, the more natural and effective it will become!

Okay, breathing might not solve all your problems, but it's a start. It puts you back in the driver's seat of those runaway feelings. But what if your body is totally freaking out too? Don't worry, we've got tools for that. Next up: how to anchor yourself back to the present moment with grounding techniques.

## IN ACTION: THE SKEPTIC TURNED BELIEVER

Michael rolled his eyes whenever anyone suggested "just taking a few deep breaths" to deal with stress. Like that was going to magically fix his problems! But one day, in the middle of a minor freak-out about an upcoming test, he figured, "What have I got to lose?" He closed his eyes and tried that box breathing thing his therapist mentioned. To his surprise, after a few minutes, his heart wasn't pounding so hard, and his mind felt a little less jumbled. It didn't make the anxiety disappear, but it made it manageable enough to get back to studying.

## PARENT TIP: BREATHE CALMLY YOURSELF

- **Be Open About Your Own Stress:** Instead of hiding it, try saying "Whoa, I need a minute to reset" then do a simple box

- ✓ Narrate the Chill: Talk through it as you breathe: "Shoulders are relaxing, the mind feels a bit clearer..." This shows them the mind-body connection.

- ✓ Make it a Mini-Ritual: Taking a few mindful breaths together before bed or during a stressful day can create a sense of calm togetherness.

# BACK TO THE NOW: GROUNDING TECHNIQUES THAT WORK

Remember how your breath goes haywire when anxiety hits? Sometimes, your body gets way too invested in the panic party too. Your heart's racing, you feel shaky, maybe even like the room is spinning. It's like your brain and body are stuck on a runaway train of freak-out, and that's definitely not helpful when you're trying to give a presentation or just chill at a party.

That's where grounding techniques come in! Grounding means using your senses to bring your focus back to the present moment. It helps calm your body and mind when you're feeling anxious. They're like an emergency brake, helping you slow down that runaway train and get back to reality.

Why does this matter? When you're super anxious, your brain's a total drama queen. It's either obsessing over some worst-case scenario that might never happen or replaying some embarrassing thing from ages ago that literally no one else remembers. Grounding helps break that cycle, reminding you of what's actually happening right here, right now.

The simplest grounding techniques use your five senses. Here's the idea: tune into one sense at a time, noticing the little details around you. This might sound too simple, but trust me, it's incredibly powerful for shifting your focus away from that anxious spiral.

**Try These:**
- **5-4-3-2-1:** Look around and name 5 things you see, 4 things you hear, 3 things you can touch, 2 things you smell, and 1 thing you can taste.

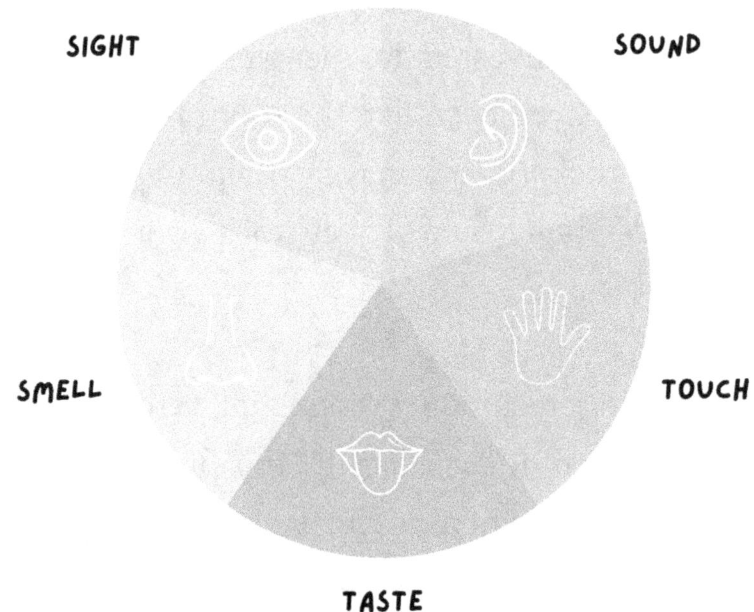

- **The Texture Hunt:** Pick up a familiar object (your phone, a pencil). Close your eyes and focus on how it feels in your hand. Is it rough? Smooth? Cold? Warm?
- **Body Scan:** Lie down or sit comfortably. Bring your attention to different parts of your body, noticing any sensations (tight shoulders, tingling fingers, etc.) without judging them.

The goal isn't to make anxiety disappear with a poof (wouldn't that be nice?). It's about creating a little space between you and those intense feelings. Grounding can help bring your system down a few notches. It's a tool to use in the middle of those anxiety waves, along with your mindful breathing and mind-surfing skills. And hey, practice makes it even more powerful! Even a few minutes of grounding each day can make a big difference when those anxious moments hit.

Grounding helps you deal with those tough moments, but anxiety often has a deeper side. That feeling of not being good enough, or constantly worrying about what others think... that needs more than a quick fix. Let's talk about how to be kinder to yourself because you deserve it.

## EXERCISE 10: GROUNDING SCAVENGER HUNT 

✓ Challenge: Sometimes, the best way to break free from an anxious spiral is to shift your focus to the here and now. This scavenger hunt turns grounding into a fun challenge!

✓ How to Play:

1. Pick Your Mission: Choose one (or do both for extra grounding power!):
   - Texture Quest: Create a list of different textures to find: something soft, something rough, something smooth, something bumpy, etc.
   - Other: Get creative! A scent scavenger hunt, a sound-focused mission, a mindful movement challenge...the possibilities are endless!
2. Get Hunting! Set a timer for 5-10 minutes and see how many items on your list you can find. As you find each one, purposely engage that sense:
   - Touch: Close your eyes and really feel the texture.
   - Sight: Spend a few moments taking in the details of the item.

✓ The Benefits:

- It forces you to tune into the present moment instead of those racing thoughts.
- Makes grounding more playful and less intimidating.
- Turns your own home into a treasure trove of calming sensations.

# CHAPTER 5:

# CHILL VIBES ONLY: BEING KIND TO YOURSELF

Ever feel like you have a bully living in your head? It whispers that you're not good enough, that you're going to embarrass yourself, and loves to remind you of past awkward moments. Ugh, who needs that negativity? Dealing with social anxiety is tough enough without putting yourself down too.

In this chapter, we're learning to fight back against that inner critic and treat ourselves with kindness. Get ready for tools to challenge those mean thoughts and replace them with the same compassion you'd show a struggling friend. We'll even cover how to handle those cringey shame spirals that can happen after an embarrassing situation. Think of this as training to be your own #1 cheerleader – because you absolutely deserve to feel good about yourself!

# BEATING UP ON YOURSELF: WHY IT'S GOTTA STOP

You know that voice in your head? The one that loves to play your personal blooper reel, focusing on every mistake, every awkward moment? It's like having a mean commentator narrating your life, and let's be real, it makes dealing with anxiety ten times harder.

Here's the thing about that voice: it's a total drama queen, always exaggerating. One tiny slip-up, and suddenly it's the end of the world. You forget one line in a presentation? You're convinced you're a total failure. Say something slightly weird in a conversation? Cue the inner voice whispering, "Everyone thinks you're a loser now."

Sometimes, being hard on ourselves feels normal. We live in a world obsessed with perfection – the perfect grades, the perfect social media feed... it's easy to feel "less than". When you're already anxious, it's even easier to fall into the trap of thinking you're never good enough. That inner critic might even feel like it's protecting you – pushing you to do better. But the truth is, it does the opposite.

That negative self-talk fuels your anxiety. It makes you afraid to try new things, speak up, or put yourself out there – because what if you mess up and that voice gets even louder? It also makes those anxious moments way worse. Imagine trying to calm down during a panic attack when your inner critic is having a field day. Not exactly helpful!

Learning to quiet that inner critic is essential for managing anxiety, and honestly, it'll make your whole life better. Here's the good news: that voice doesn't have to control you. Think of self-compassion as your superpower against that negativity. It's time to start talking to yourself the way you'd talk to a friend who's struggling. Because guess what? You deserve that same kindness and support.

That negative inner voice makes managing anxiety so much harder. The truth is, you deserve the same kindness you'd give anyone else. Let's start treating yourself with the respect and encouragement you need to thrive.

## IN ACTION: THE POST-PARTY SPIRAL 

Emily always looked forward to parties, but the moment she got home, the fun would crash. Her inner critic would replay every slightly awkward thing she said or did on loop. "Why did I tell that story? It was so dumb!" or "Did I laugh too loud? Everyone probably thinks I'm annoying." These thoughts would spiral, making her convinced that no one at the party actually liked her. Learning about self-compassion was a game-changer. Instead of letting her inner critic run wild, she started asking herself: "Would I talk to a friend this way about one awkward moment?" She began to see how those thoughts were distorted and didn't define her as a person. The post-party spiral didn't disappear overnight, but it became easier to manage.

## EXERCISE 11: THE THOUGHT REFRAME 

Challenge: Our inner critic can be brutal, right? This exercise will help you fight back and start building that self-compassion muscle.

✓ Instructions

1. Catch the Critic: Pay attention to your self-talk for a day or two. When you hear that negative inner voice pop up, jot it down. (Ex: "I'm so awkward!", "What a loser...", "I'll never get this right!")

2. Reality Check: Pick one of those harsh thoughts. Ask yourself these questions:
   - Is this thought 100% true, or am I exaggerating?
   - Would I say this to a friend who made the same mistake?
   - Is this helping me or making me feel worse?

3. Find the Reframe: Try to rewrite that thought in a kinder, more realistic way. Here are some examples and starters to help you:
   - Instead of: "I'm so stupid, I totally messed that up." Try: "That was tricky, and it's okay to make mistakes. I'm still learning."
   - Instead of: "Everyone's laughing at me." Try: "I don't actually know what they're thinking. They might not even have noticed."

✓ **The Power of Practice:** This won't be an overnight fix, but the more you practice reframing those negative thoughts, the easier it becomes. Think of it as training your brain to be kinder to yourself!

|  The Critic's Corner  |  Reality Check  |
| --- | --- |
|  |  |
|  |  |
|  |  |
|  |  |
|  |  |
|  |  |
|  |  |
|  |  |

# SELF-COMPASSION HACKS: YOUR INNER CHEERLEADER

Okay, we've talked about how to ditch that mean inner critic who loves making you miserable. Now it's time to replace it with something much better: Your Inner Cheerleader! Imagine having a friend who constantly put you down, and made you feel bad about every little mistake – would you keep them around? Heck no! So, why do we put up with that voice in our heads?

Self-compassion is basically being as nice to yourself as you would be to a friend who's struggling. It means cutting yourself some slack, recognizing that you're not perfect (because guess what, no one is!), and talking to yourself with support rather than judgment. Remember how that harsh inner critic fuels your anxiety? Self-compassion does the opposite. It helps you bounce back from those awkward moments without spiraling into self-doubt. It makes it easier to silence those "I'm not good enough" worry scripts. And when you do have an anxiety flare-up, being kind to yourself instead of beating yourself up can make those tough moments a little less intense.

Sometimes people worry that self-compassion is like being self-centered or letting yourself off the hook. But that's not true at all. In fact, it gives you the strength to actually try new things, face challenges, and grow as a person. When you believe in yourself (even with flaws!), it's way easier to step outside your comfort zone.

Training your Inner Cheerleader takes some practice, but it gets easier over time. And trust me, it'll change your relationship with anxiety, and honestly, your whole life. Let's get started on some self-compassion hacks! Even small steps towards being kinder to yourself make a difference, especially in those moments when shame tries to take over. Let's talk about how to handle those extra-tough feelings.

- ✓ **Acknowledge the Struggle:** When they berate themselves, point out how hard they're trying. "Learning to be nicer to yourself is tough work!" This validates their feelings, not the harsh self-talk.

- ✓ **Praise the Imperfect Effort:** Focus on attempts at self-kindness ("I love hearing you say 'it's okay to make mistakes' to yourself"). This matters, even if their inner critic is still loud.
- ✓ **Remind Them They're Not Alone:** Share a time you were hard on yourself, and how you learned to shift that. Knowing others get it boosts their own sense of hope.

# HANDLING SHAME SPIRALS: WHEN IT FEELS EXTRA AWFUL

We've talked about that mean inner critic, right? Well, shame is like its evil twin. It's that sinking feeling in your stomach after you say something embarrassing, that feeling like everyone's secretly judging you, the voice in your head making you feel like you messed up so badly you just want to disappear.

Shame is a normal human emotion, but man, does it feel awful! And for teens with anxiety, it's basically rocket fuel. Sometimes, the worry about feeling judged can become so intense that it spirals into a full-blown panic attack. Or, when something embarrassing does happen, shame can take over, making you replay the moment on a loop, convincing yourself no one will ever like you again (spoiler alert: not true!).

Often, the feelings of shame aren't just about what happened. It taps into our deepest fears – of being unlikable, not good enough, not belonging. Especially as a teen, when fitting in can feel like everything, those shame spirals can hit extra hard.

The good news is, you don't have to let shame control you. While you might not be able to make those feelings vanish, there are ways to break those spirals and lessen their power. Let's tackle this step-by-step. First, it's about recognizing what shame feels like in your body and learning how to separate yourself from that awful feeling. And then, we'll work on challenging those shame-fueled thoughts with some self-compassion (your armor against that inner critic!) and a dose of reality.

Okay, I know those shame spirals feel impossible to escape. But there are ways to slow them down, separate yourself from those harsh thoughts, and find a bit of calm. Mindfulness techniques, even simple ones, can give you back some control. Let's talk about how to make mindfulness work for you.

## IN ACTION: THE BLUSHING BLUNDER 

Every time Michael was called on in class, his face would turn bright red. It felt like a spotlight was on him, and he was sure everyone was secretly laughing. The thought "They all think I'm weird" would loop in his head. He started avoiding raising his hand, even when he knew the answer, and his grades started to slip because of it. Learning to challenge that thought ("They're judging me" ) and using some calming techniques (like focusing on his breath for a few seconds) made a huge difference. Turns out, most people were too focused on themselves to even notice his blushing, and it faded way faster than he thought it did.

## EXERCISE 12: TREAT YOURSELF LIKE A FRIEND 

✓ Challenge: Sometimes when shame hits, we talk to ourselves in a way we'd never talk to a friend. This exercise flips that around, helping you access that compassion you have for others!

✓ Instructions:

1. Remember the Shame: Think of a recent time you felt a strong pang of shame. Maybe you messed up on a presentation, had an awkward moment at a party, whatever it was, write a few sentences describing it.

2. Imagine It's Your Friend: Pretend a friend comes to you feeling terrible about the exact same situation. What would you say? Write them a response filled with kindness, support, and a dose of perspective. Focus on what you value about them as a person and remind them that one moment doesn't define them.

3. Now, It's Your Turn: Reread what you wrote to your "friend". Can you offer even a little bit of that same kindness to yourself? Try rewriting some of those key phrases addressing yourself directly. ("You're a good person, and everyone makes mistakes..." )

Inner Critic's Voice          Friend Mode Activated

# MINDFUL MOMENTS: BEYOND JUST MEDITATION

Okay, "mindfulness" might sound like something you do in yoga class with your eyes closed and weird chanting. But it's way more than that. It's basically training your brain to chill in the present moment, so you're not always lost in a tornado of worries. Seriously, our brains love to freak out about the past ("Why did I say that stupid thing yesterday?") or the future ("What if I totally embarrass myself at the party?"). This is like pouring gasoline on the fire of anxiety. Mindfulness helps you build that "focus muscle" so you can bring your brain back to what's actually happening right now.

**Mindfulness can be super simple:**
- Taking a walk and actually paying attention to the sights, sounds, smells around you, instead of obsessing over that text you wish you hadn't sent.
- Truly focusing on the taste of a snack and enjoying it, instead of mindlessly munching while scrolling social media.
- When that cringey thought about yesterday pops into your head, acknowledging it and then letting it drift away (like watching a cloud float by), instead of getting all tangled up in it.
- Ditch your phone for a few minutes and take a walk outside. Pay close attention to what you see — the colors of leaves, the textures of

buildings – and the sounds around you. Nature is the best for this!

- Pick a boring chore and turn it into a mindfulness challenge. Really focus on every step – the feeling of the warm water when washing dishes, the rhythm of folding clothes.
- After being on your phone, close your eyes for one minute and just breathe. This breaks that scrolling daze and helps you transition mindfully to the next thing.

Look, mindfulness isn't a magic anxiety eraser. But it does change the game! You get better at focusing on the present, not those "what if" disasters your brain loves to invent. It also makes it easier to hear those mean self-critic thoughts without letting them take over. And guess what? Those social skills we're about to dive into? Way easier to rock when you're mindful of what's going on in your own head.

We've talked about how mindfulness helps you take charge of your thoughts and feelings, even in those anxiety-provoking moments. Turns out, this is like your secret weapon for navigating the crazy world of socializing. Ready to boost those conversation skills and find your social superpowers?

## IN ACTION: THE OVERTHINKER

Emily was the queen of overthinking. After every conversation, she'd torture herself, replaying every single word, wondering if she sounded dumb or if the other person secretly hated her now. It was exhausting! Learning some mindfulness techniques changed everything. Taking a mindful walk, focusing on the sights and sounds around her, helped her step outside those obsessive thought loops. Or, a quick body scan, bringing attention to the sensations in her body, grounded her in the present moment

## EXERCISE 13: THE MINDFUL SNACK ATTACK

✓ Challenge: Ready to turn snack time into a mindfulness workout? You'll need:

- A favorite snack (something small is best, like a piece of candy or a few berries)
- A quiet place, free from distractions

✓ Instructions:

1. Behold the Snack: Take a moment to really look at your snack. Notice its colors, its shape, any textures you can see.
2. Sniff It Out: Now, bring it up to your nose and take a whiff. What do you smell? Is it sweet, savory, fruity?

3. Feel the Texture: Before popping it in your mouth, take a second to feel it. Is it smooth, rough, squishy?

4. Tasting Time: Now, take a small bite. Don't chomp down and swallow! Roll it around on your tongue. Notice the flavors, and the way the texture changes in your mouth.

5. Mindful Munching: Keep going slowly and mindfully until your snack is gone.

✓ The Power of Slowing Down: This might seem silly, but it's a powerful way to practice mindfulness. Most of the time, we shovel food into our mouths without even thinking. This exercise helps you tune in to the present moment and actually enjoy what you're eating.

Part 3:

# SOCIAL SKILLS NINJA SCHOOL

# INSIDE THIS PART

Ready to ditch those awkward vibes and own your social life? Consider this section your secret weapon for becoming a social butterfly (or just comfortably navigating those gotta-be-there situations). We're about to level up your conversation game, find your people, and even learn to laugh off those cringey moments – because hey, awkwardness happens to the best of us!

Social Skills Ninja School isn't about becoming someone you're not. It's about tapping into the awesome person you already are! We'll cover everything from small talk that doesn't make you want to crawl under a rock to truly listening in a way that makes people feel seen. You'll learn how to spot genuine friends, bounce back from rejection like a champ, and walk into a room full of strangers with your head held high (even if you're secretly shaking on the inside). Get ready to unlock your social superpowers and become a force to be reckoned with!

# CHAPTER 6:

## SMALL TALK, BIG WINS: STARTING THE CONVO

Small talk. Ugh. For anyone with social anxiety, it might as well be a form of torture! But guess what? Even those seemingly pointless chats are your key to unlocking better connections.

This chapter is your small-talk survival guide! We're ditching those awkward "What's up?" moments and learning how to start real conversations without feeling like you want to vanish into thin air. You'll get go-to questions that actually spark interesting convos, plus the secret skill that makes you super likable: truly listening.

Level up time! No more dreading those gotta-talk-to-someone moments. Get ready to handle small talk with confidence – and maybe even discover you kinda enjoy it!

# CONVO STARTERS THAT DON'T MAKE YOU CRINGE

Small talk. For many teens, it's basically torture. You want to connect with people, but the thought of starting a conversation makes you want to disappear into a poof of smoke. What if you say something dumb? What if there's an awkward silence and the other person thinks you're a total loser?

Here's the deal: good conversation starters are like cheat codes for beating social anxiety. They make breaking the ice way less stressful. And guess what? You don't need to be some naturally hilarious, super-smooth charmer. Think of it like opening a door – you just need a little nudge to get started, and then hopefully the conversation can flow.

Let's stock your social toolkit with some simple (but not lame!) openers:

- **The Compliment + Question Combo:** Notice something cool about the person (their shirt, their awesome art project, etc.). Follow a genuine compliment with a question like, "Love those sneakers! Where'd you get them?".
- **The Shared Experience Opener:** Bond over something happening around you. In class, it could be, "Is this test going to be as brutal as I think it is?". At a party, try "This playlist is awesome, know any other bands like this?".

- **Asking for a Tiny Favor:** It sounds weird, but it works! Ask to borrow a pencil, ask for directions (even if you know them), or "Could you grab me a napkin?". It's a low-pressure way to start an interaction.
- **The Pop Culture Connection:** Reference something that's trending. ("Did you see that crazy meme?" or "Think you could survive on that new reality show?"). These are easy since everyone's likely got an opinion.
- **The Hypothetical Hero:** Ask a playful, out-of-the-box question. ("If you could have any superpower for one day, what would it be?" or "If you were stranded on a deserted island and could only bring 3 things, what would you choose?"). It gets them thinking and shows your fun side.
- **The "Help Me Out" Opener:** Ask for a recommendation. ("Got any good book suggestions?" or "Know any decent places to get pizza around here?"). It's flattering and sparks an easy convo around their interests.

Remember, open-ended questions are your friend! These get more than a yes/no answer and keep things flowing. Instead of "Do you like this song?", try "What other music are you into lately?". Also, actually listening to the other person is key – it's about connecting, not just hearing yourself talk. And finally, chill out (even if you have to fake it!). Relaxed vibes are way more appealing than someone who's trying too hard. Everyone gets awkward sometimes! The more you practice these openers, the easier it becomes to kickstart those convos without the cringe.

It's important to understand that conversation is a two-way street. Don't feel pressured to be the only one making it happen. If you try a few of these openers, and the other person gives short, uninterested answers or doesn't ask anything back, it's okay to back off. Maybe they're super shy, having a bad day, or simply not interested in chatting. Don't take it personally! Trying to force a conversation can feel even more awkward than a little silence. Sometimes, respecting the other person's social energy is the kindest thing you can do for both of you.

Okay, so you're mastering the art of starting convos. But what about the actual talking part? Turns out, that being a good listener is a secret superpower. It makes the other person feel seen and shows you're genuinely interested. Ready to level up those listening skills?

IN ACTION: FROM INVISIBLE TO INCLUDED

Parties were Michael's worst nightmare. He'd stand awkwardly by the snack table, wishing the floor would swallow him whole. He wanted to connect with people, but the thought of starting a conversation was paralyzing. Practicing the "shared experience" opener was a lifesaver. Noticing something happening around him ("This song is a banger, you know who this is?" or "Did you see Emily's epic faceplant earlier?") made those first few words way easier. Turns out, people are happy to chat when you give them a simple opening!

# LISTENER = SUPERHERO: TRICKS TO ACTUALLY ENJOY TALKING

Okay, we've tackled starting conversations. But what about the actual talking part? Turns out, being a good listener is your secret weapon for navigating the social world. Why? Because people LOVE to talk about themselves (newsflash!). Giving someone your full attention is like the ultimate compliment. They feel seen, they feel valued. Plus, when you actually listen, you might be surprised by what you learn – shared interests, hilarious stories, and maybe even get a hot tip on the best pizza place in town. And the best part? It takes the pressure off YOU to fill every second with something super clever.

So, how do you level up those listening skills? Here's the deal:

- **Ditch the Distractions:** Put your phone down (for real!), make eye contact, and actually be present.
- **Body Language Matters:** Nodding, leaning in a little, and keeping your arms uncrossed shows you're totally engaged.
- **Become a Question Ninja:** Instead of just waiting for your turn to talk, ask them to elaborate on what they're saying. ("OMG, your goldfish stole your sandwich? Tell me more!").
- **Focus on the Speaker:** Focusing on your own thoughts can make it hard to truly listen, which can stall the conversation. Be genuinely curious and ask follow-up questions. This shows you care about what they have to say and makes the interaction more enjoyable for both of you.
- **The Power of Reflection:** Try summarizing what you're hearing them say in your own words ("Okay, so it sounds like you're feeling kinda nervous about that big test."). This shows you get it.
- **Chill Vibes Only:** Even if you don't completely agree with everything they say, keep an open mind. Being a good listener is about connecting, not about always being right.

Being truly interested in what someone has to say makes them like you more. It builds trust and makes those connections feel genuine. People will want to be around you because they know they can just be themselves. And hey, those conversations actually become enjoyable instead of a total stress-fest!

Speaking of genuine connections... Being a good listener helps you spot those people worth having in your corner. But what exactly should you look for in a true friend? That's in the next section.

## EXERCISE 14: THE INTEREST INTERVIEW

✓ **Challenge:** Think you know your parents or siblings really well? This exercise might surprise you! Turns out, even the people we live with have hidden passions, funny stories, and perspectives we might not even know about. Here's the challenge:

✓ **Pick Your Interviewee:** Choose a family member you'd like to get to know better. It could be a parent, grandparent, sibling, or even a cousin you see often!

✓ **Prep Your Questions:** Think about what you're genuinely curious about. Instead of the usual "How was your day?" try questions like:
- What's one hobby you've always wanted to try?
- Tell me about your favorite childhood memory.
- If you could go back in time, what advice would you give your teenage self?

✓ **The Interview:**
- Find a time when you both can relax, free of distractions.

- Explain this is a fun "get to know you" project.
- Actively listen to their answers! (Use those skills we talked about). Ask follow-up questions if something intrigues you.

✓ What's Next:

- Reflect: Did anything surprise you about their answers? Did you learn something totally new?
- Share: If they're comfortable with it, share what you learned about them with another family member, showing how much you were paying attention!
- Keep It Going!: This could become a fun tradition, helping you build a stronger connection with your family.

# CHAPTER 7:

# FINDING YOUR PEOPLE (AND WHAT TO DO IF YOU LOSE THEM)

Finding your people – the ones who get your weird humor, support your passions, and always have your back – is the BEST! But when you've got social anxiety, it can feel impossible to put yourself out there and build those awesome friendships.

This chapter is your friendship roadmap! We'll figure out how to spot those genuine connections and ditch the fake friends. You'll learn tips for keeping those awesome friendships going strong (because hey, even good things take work sometimes!) And we're gonna tackle those painful rejection moments– because they happen– and how to bounce back like a champ. Get ready to find your crew and build the kind of friendships that make life way more fun!

# THE FRIEND FILTER: WHAT REAL CONNECTION LOOKS LIKE

Okay, so you're mastering those social skills – starting convos, and being a good listener. Amazing! But how do you know if someone's actually worth your time and energy? Not everyone you chat with is destined to be your bestie. So, what does a real, healthy friendship actually look like?

Sure, having a good time is a major part of friendship. But think beyond just shared inside jokes and weekend plans. Real friends have the deeper stuff too:

- **Support Squad:** They celebrate your wins and help you through the rough patches. You know you can count on them, no matter what.
- **The Honesty Zone:** True friends aren't afraid to tell you when you're messing up (in a kind way!). They care enough to help you grow as a person.
- **Respect = Non-Negotiable:** They value your opinions, even when they disagree. No teasing that actually hurts, no pressuring you to do stuff you don't want to do.
- **Team Reciprocity:** Friendship is a two-way street. Both people put in effort, make time for each other, and genuinely care how the other is doing.

So, as you're expanding your social circle, ask yourself some important questions. How does this person make me feel? Do I feel energized and happy around them, or do they make me anxious? Do they seem to bring out the best in me? Is this someone who's interested in hearing about my life, or do I find myself always playing the therapist role? Is the overall vibe light and fun, or are there streaks of unnecessary drama and competition?

Watch out for those red flags that signal unhealthy friendships: people who only reach out when they need a favor, who subtly try to tear you down, or who thrive on gossip and trash-talking.

Always remember: you get to set the standards for who you call "friend." Don't lower the bar just to avoid being alone. It might take some time to find your tribe, but having real, supportive friends by your side makes life a whole lot sweeter.

Having those deep connections is amazing, but let's be real – friendships aren't always sunshine and rainbows. There might be times when someone lets you down, or you say the wrong thing. Learning how to handle those bumps in the road is just as important as finding your squad in the first place.

## IN ACTION: SETTING HEALTHY BOUNDARIES

- **The Honest but Kind Friend.** Michael genuinely liked hanging out with Jake. Jake was the life of the party, always cracking jokes... but sometimes his ideas were reckless. One night, Jake wanted to spray paint a grumpy neighbor's fence, Michael knew this was a terrible plan with serious consequences. Instead of blindly following, Michael refused to go along and tried to talk sense into Jake. Jake got annoyed, but Michael stood his ground, caring enough about his friend (and himself) to avoid a stupid decision.

- **The Reciprocity Fail.** Anna always wanted to talk – about her latest crush, her friend drama, anything and everything. The problem was, that she rarely seemed interested in hearing what Lisa had to say. Whenever Lisa tried to share, Anna would quickly turn the conversation back to herself. Lisa tried giving subtle hints but nothing worked. She started to dread their conversations, feeling like she was just a sounding board,  not a true friend. This wasn't the kind of balanced friendship she wanted.

# BOUNCE BACK: WHEN FRIENDSHIPS FIZZLE (AND WHAT TO DO)

Friendship is awesome when it's working, but what about when it's...not? It's a hard truth, but sometimes friendships change, or straight-up fade away. Maybe you and your bestie since elementary school suddenly realize you have nothing in common anymore. Maybe there was that big fight that no one really recovered from. Or worse, a friend who used to have your back now hangs with a group of people who always made you feel like an outsider. Ouch.

It doesn't matter if it happens gradually or in one dramatic blow-up, losing a friend hurts. Sometimes a lot. You might feel confused, angry, maybe even a little betrayed. On top of that, it's easy for those anxious thoughts to take over: "Am I unlikeable? Will I ever find real friends?"

Here's the thing to remember: friendships, just like any relationship, require effort from both sides and sometimes circumstances or people change. That doesn't mean there's something wrong with YOU.

Let's unpack how to handle those fizzling friendships with a dose of reality and a plan to move forward:

- **Step 1: Give Yourself Space To Feel It.** Don't try to force yourself to be all "whatever, I didn't need them anyway" right away. Bottling up those emotions will just make them explode later. Let yourself be sad, disappointed, or angry for a while. Talk to someone you trust, crank up some sad songs, and have a good cry if you need to.
- **Step 2: Is It Fixable (And Do You Want To)?** Sometimes a little honest conversation can get things back on track. If it's a close friend and there was a misunderstanding, consider reaching out to clear the air. But sometimes, you've both just grown in different directions. Or, if the friendship was becoming toxic, letting it fade might be the healthiest choice.
- **Step 3: Don't Take It Personally (Easier Said Than Done).** This is where those anxiety thoughts can really mess with you. Remember, the friendship ending doesn't equal YOU being unworthy. People

change, interests shift – life takes you on different paths.

- **Step 4: Focus On Your True Tribe.** Losing a friend can shine a light on those who truly are your people. Spend more time with friends who uplift you, have your back, and make you feel good about yourself. And remember, there are awesome new connections waiting to be made too!

**Bonus Tip:** If a former friend is intentionally being nasty or spreading rumors, don't engage. Walk away with your head high. Their drama isn't worth your energy. Dealing with fading friendships is part of growing up, and it gets easier with practice. The more you focus on building strong, genuine connections, the less power those fizzled friendships have over you.

Remember, one rejection doesn't define you. Dust yourself off, hold your head high, and get ready to step out of your comfort zone, because who knows what awesome (or hilariously awkward) experiences await at that next party?

## EXERCISE 15: FRIENDSHIP REFLECTIONS

✓ Challenge: Losing a friend can feel like a punch in the gut, even if the friendship was fading. But even tough experiences are opportunities for growth. Take some time to reflect with these questions:

- What did I learn about what I want from friends?
- Were there qualities this friend had that I really valued (loyalty, good listener, etc.)?
- Were there things that drained me (constant negativity, flakiness, etc.)?
- What kind of support did I need from this friend that I didn't get?
- Could I have handled any parts differently? Don't beat yourself up, but be honest: Were there times I could've communicated better, been a more supportive friend, or set clearer boundaries? This is about learning for future friendships, not assigning blame.
- What are the positive things I'll take from it? Even difficult friendships can teach us something. Maybe you learned that you're funnier than you thought, discovered a shared interest that led you to a new hobby, or even learned how to stand up for yourself.

✓ Remember: It's okay to grieve the loss of a friendship. But also recognize that the lessons you learn from this experience will help you build even stronger, healthier connections in the future!

# CHAPTER 8:

# PARTY MODE ACTIVATED: OWNING THE ROOM (OKAY, MAYBE JUST A CORNER)

Parties, group hangouts, big events... They can feel like major boss battles for anyone with social anxiety. The idea of entering a room full of people? Nope! But here's the deal: you don't have to become the life of the party to handle those situations.

This chapter is about finding your own version of "party mode." We'll cover how to mentally prepare when you know you'll be in a crowd (even when you'd rather hide). You'll learn tricks for feeling more comfortable in those overwhelming social settings, and how to make a graceful exit when you've hit your limit. Think of it as unlocking the confidence to own those spaces – even if it's just finding a chill corner to hang in for a bit!

# GET YOUR HEAD IN THE GAME (EVEN WHEN YOU DON'T WANT TO)

Okay, let's get real. Some days the idea of facing a crowd (especially one filled with your peers) feels like climbing a mountain in flip-flops...while everyone's watching. That sick feeling in your stomach? The voice in your head screaming "Stay home!"? Totally normal, especially when you're dealing with anxiety on top of the crazy rollercoaster that is being a teenager.

But here's the thing: hiding under the covers isn't a long-term solution. If you want to go to parties, hang with friends, or even just make it through the school day without wanting to disappear, you've gotta find a way to work with your brain, not against it.

Think of this section as your super-secret training plan for tackling those anxiety triggers. We're not going to force you to be the center of attention right away (unless you're into that, then go for it!). Start small, like a ninja in training. Instead of bailing completely, try for a quick "hello" to that kid in your science class, or actually ask your teacher that question you've been dying to know. Every little win chips away at those "I can't" thoughts.

**Party Prep:** It's Not Just About the Outfit: Sure, picking something you feel good in helps, but the real power move is taming those pre-party jitters. When your mind spirals with "what ifs?" and worst-case scenarios, it's hard to even get out the door. Try calming your body down first — deep breaths, a short walk outside, or even busting some silly moves to your favorite song. Then challenge those negative thoughts head-on. Instead of "I'm going to embarrass myself", try "Maybe, maybe not, but I can handle it." Remember, the hardest part is often taking that first step. One small act of bravery makes the next one a little bit easier!

**Survival Kit Mode Activated:** Picture having a metaphorical backpack filled with tools to manage those panic attacks in the moment. Here's what to stash in yours:

## SOCIAL SURVIVOR KIT BACKPACK

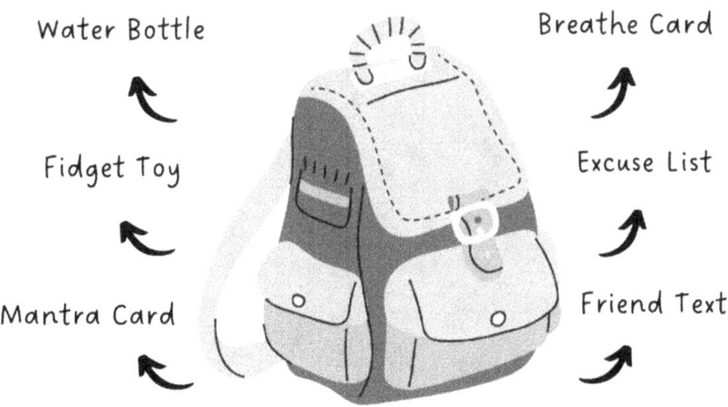

- **Calming/Breathe Card:** Lists a quick breathing exercise or grounding technique.
- **Excuse List:** A few pre-written excuses for leaving ("Need some air", "Gotta find my friend").
- **Friend Text/Alert:** A reminder to text a trusted friend/parent if anxiety is overwhelming.
- **Water Bottle:** Staying hydrated helps with physical and mental stress.
- **Fidget Toy:** A small fidget toy for redirecting nervous energy.
- **Mindful Mantra (Mantra card):** A positive phrase to repeat silently ("I'm safe", "This will pass").

Here's the deal: your brain is incredible...but sometimes it's a total drama queen! That voice inside your head whispering, "Everyone will laugh at you" or "You're gonna totally mess this up"? That's your inner critic getting way too creative. Don't let those negative thoughts win! Reframe them: "Feeling nervous is normal", "I can handle this", or even the classic "Fake it till you make it!" Heck, give your inner critic a silly name (more on that later!) – mine's Karen and she seriously needs to CHILL.

Of course, even the pros fumble sometimes. That's why having a few "escape routes" ready is a smart strategy! Time to master the art of a clean getaway...

## PARENT TIP: PREPPING WITHOUT PRESSURE 

✓ Focus on the Controllables. Instead of trying to predict the outcome, talk about what they CAN prepare for – knowing where they're going, what to wear, etc. Practicality reduces the overwhelm.

✓ Normalize Some Nerves: Saying "It's okay to feel a bit jittery, most people do in new situations" lets them know they're not weird for feeling anxious.

✓ One Goal is Enough: Pick one small, achievable social goal for the event ("I'll make eye contact with two people"). This gives them a focus without demanding perfection.

## IN ACTION: ANNA'S PARTY PANIC 

Anna had been dreading Emily's party for weeks. The idea of walking into a room full of people she barely knew filled her with a familiar wave of nausea. Her inner critic was in full "disaster movie" mode: "You'll say something stupid, trip on the rug, EVERYONE will laugh..." Her first instinct was to text a fake sick excuse and hide.

But...she'd been practicing those thought-challenging techniques. "Okay", she told herself, "Feeling nervous is normal. I don't have to be the center of attention, maybe I can just say hi to Emily and a few people." She spent some time planning her outfit (something comfortable = one less thing to stress about) and even practiced a few conversation starters in the mirror.

On the day of the party, the jitters were still there, but they didn't feel quite as overwhelming. Anna reminded herself of her small goal: just find Emily, wish her happy birthday, and maybe chat with one other person. She also gave herself permission to leave after an hour if it felt like too much. Taking that first step through the door was still hard, but it felt a tiny bit easier than she expected.

# TACTICAL RETREAT: BAILING WITHOUT THE AWKWARD

Let's be real: sometimes, the party is a nope, the school event is a nightmare, and being around people feels like running a gauntlet blindfolded. You try the pep talks, the breathing exercises... but all you want is to teleport back to your bed and hide under the covers.

Take a breath, 'cause guess what? That feeling is totally normal, and it doesn't make you a loser. Sometimes, your anxiety goes into full-blown ninja mode, and the best thing you can do is listen and give yourself a break. Pushing yourself when you're already maxed out just makes things worse. Knowing when to step back? That's an honest-to-goodness superpower.

Of course, sometimes you just gotta go. But disappearing like a wisp of smoke can create its own problems. So, here's your guide to a graceful exit:

- **The "Irish Goodbye":** The classic fade-into-the-crowd maneuver. Ideal for when you've maxed out on small talk and just need a breather.
- **"Oops, Gotta Run!":** Sometimes, a simple excuse is all it takes. "Homework emergency," "My ride is here" – keep it believable, but no need for a whole dramatic backstory.
- **The "Social Battery" Fizzle:** Honesty goes a long way. "Hey, I'm having a good time, but I'm kinda reaching my people limit. Let's catch up later?" Real friends totally get it.
- **Bounce, Don't Ghost:** Vanishing into thin air is a recipe for next-

-time awkwardness. A quick, "Had to bail early, [vague reason]" text saves the day.

- **Timing is Everything:** Don't wait until you're about to lose it. Tune into those warning signs (sweaty palms, racing thoughts). Dip out before you hit critical meltdown mode.

Remember, this isn't about being rude; it's about self-care. Knowing when to say "peace out" is a superpower, so you can recharge and come back stronger. Don't worry, that doesn't make you a loser — it makes you strategic. Ready to level up those social ninja skills even more? In the next chapter, we're tackling awkwardness head-on. Get ready to transform cringey moments into funny stories!

## IN ACTION! THE OVERSTIMULATED INTROVERT

Emily loves hanging out with her friends, but big parties always leave her feeling overwhelmed. Tonight's no different — the music's blasting, people are crammed into every corner, and she's been fielding non-stop questions and chatter for the past hour. Her mind feels like a scrambled mess, and she can't even form a coherent sentence. She spots a side door leading to a patio and uses her "grab some air" excuse to slip away. The crisp night air and a few minutes of silence are instantly calming.

She texts her best friend, "This party is nuts! Need a breather lol" just for that extra bit of connection that helps her feel less alone. Feeling recharged, she heads back inside ready to tackle the rest of the night.

## EXERCISE 16: ESCAPE ROUTE BRAINSTORM

✓ **Challenge:** Sometimes, the best way to handle a social situation is to make a graceful exit. There's no shame in needing a breather! The key is to have a few go-to phrases ready so you can handle the situation without adding extra stress.

✓ **Instructions:**

1. **Brainstorm Your Phrases:** Think of 3-5 short, believable phrases you feel comfortable saying when you need to slip away. These should be versatile enough to work in most situations.
2. **Match the Situation:** For each phrase, come up with a specific scenario where it would be the perfect escape route.

✓ **Example:**

- **Phrase:** "I'm going to get some food/a drink."
- **Situation:** Stuck in an awkward one-on-one conversation.

## Escape Line

## Scene Change

# CHAPTER 9:

# HANDLING AWKWARDNESS LIKE A PRO

Awkward moments. We've all been there – spilling your drink, blurting out something weird, walking into the wrong classroom... ugh! The cringe is enough to make you want to vanish forever. But here's the deal: awkwardness is part of life, even for the smoothest-seeming people.

This chapter is your guide to surviving (and even laughing off) those toe-curling situations. We'll cover ways to turn embarrassing blunders into funny stories, how to own those awkward moments with a dose of humor, and how to project confidence even when you're mortified inside. Think of it as unlocking superhero skills for deflecting awkwardness and owning those cringe-worthy moments like a total champ!

# LAUGH IT OFF: TURNING CRINGE MOMENTS INTO FUNNY STORIES

Okay, let's be brutally honest – even those with social skills smoother than a milkshake have those epic fail moments. You know the ones… where you trip in front of your entire class, spill a drink all over your crush, or accidentally address the principal as "Grandma." Your face blazes like a neon sign, your brain short-circuits, and all you want is for the earth to swallow you whole. In that moment, it feels like the absolute worst thing to ever happen in the history of the universe. But here's a secret weapon: laughter. Yep, transforming those cringe-worthy moments into hilarious stories is not only possible, it's how you level up your awkwardness-handling skills. Think about it – when you can find the humor in a situation, it instantly lessens its power over you. Awkwardness suddenly becomes way less intimidating. Plus, proving to yourself you can survive even the most embarrassing scenarios is a huge confidence booster. And here's the best part: those cringe-fests often become legendary inside jokes with your real friends, the ones who laugh with you, not at you.

Here's the thing: turning cringe into comedy takes a bit of practice. Start thinking like a stand-up comic:

- **Exaggerate:** The more you amp up the ridiculous details, the funnier it becomes. That trip wasn't just a stumble; you practically flew across the room!
- **Add a Soundtrack:** Every great movie has epic music. Imagine your blunder in slow motion set to the "Titanic" theme...hilarious.
- **Your Inner Voiceover:** Narrate the moment with a sarcastic, overly dramatic voice. Picture a nature documentary voice: "And here we see the rare teenager in its natural habitat, attempting a basic task...it fails spectacularly."

Need inspiration? Every awkward legend has that one infamous story. Dig into your own cringe collection and share it with a trusted friend. Add those funny twists, and soon you'll both be in stitches. The more you tell the story, the less power it holds over you.

Of course, sometimes the cringe is too intense, and even trying to laugh feels impossible. That's okay! Acknowledge the suckiness, ride out the temporary wave of awkwardness, and give yourself permission to feel it. You can still find the humor later when it doesn't sting quite as much.

Laughing at yourself is a superpower. It shows the world (and that pesky inner critic) that you won't let embarrassing moments define you. That, my friend, is what true chill looks like. Now, start collecting those cringey moments – they might just become your best comedy material yet! After all, if you can't laugh at yourself, then who can you laugh at? Sometimes a good chuckle is the best way to move on. But what if the cringe was a bit too intense for just a giggle? Next up: Damage Control – when to address the awkwardness head-on and when to simply let it fade away.

## PARENT TIP: SMALL TALK, BIG WINS

- ✓ **Resist the Swoop-In:** It's SO tempting to rescue teens in uncomfortable moments. But waiting a beat allows them to work it out themselves, building confidence.

- ✓ **Debrief, Don't Critique:** Later, ask open-ended questions: "That seemed tricky, what was going on for you?", "Want to brainstorm how you might handle it next time?". This is about problem-solving, not shame.

✓ Praise the Effort: Acknowledge how hard it is to push outside their comfort zone, regardless of how smoothly the interaction went. This reinforces brave social behavior.

**IN ACTION: THE WARDROBE MALFUNCTION**

Biggest presentation of my life. I spent days choosing the perfect outfit, ironing it to perfection, feeling like a million bucks. As I walk confidently to the front of the class, I hear a horrifying ripping sound. My pants split right down the middle! My heart dropped, and I could feel my face turning bright red. But then, a spark of defiance kicked in. I winked at my friends in the front row and said, "Guess distressed jeans are in even for presentations now!" I totally owned the ripped pants look for the rest of the presentation, even throwing in a few model-like poses. Sure, it wasn't what I planned, but hey, sometimes you gotta improvise and turn embarrassment into an opportunity to shine.

# DAMAGE CONTROL: WHEN TO ADDRESS THE AWKWARDNESS HEAD-ON



Okay, even after you've mastered laughing off the cringey moments, there are those awkward situations that go beyond funny and land squarely in "Oh no, did I really just do/say that?!" territory. We're talking about accidentally insulting someone, creating a whole misunderstanding, or having a full-on meltdown in front of your crush. Ouch.

The first step to damage control is figuring out whether it's better to address the awkwardness head-on or strategically let it fade into the background. If you've genuinely hurt someone's feelings, even if it was completely unintentional, a sincere "I'm sorry, that didn't come out right" can prevent a bigger fallout. Did your comment get totally misinterpreted? A simple "Oops, I think we got our wires crossed, let me clarify..." can stop things from spiraling. Sometimes the awkwardness is so obvious everyone's thinking about it. Briefly acknowledging it with a lighthearted "Well, that was awkward..." can actually break the tension and get everyone laughing.

**Let It Fade When:**
- **Minor Slip-Up:** Spilled a tiny bit of water? Tripped but recovered quickly? Most people won't even remember those moments.
- **The Overthink Spiral:** The more you replay the awkwardness in your head, the worse it seems. Sometimes distraction is the best medicine.
- **Everyone Else Moved On:** If the moment passed and the conversation shifted, trying to revisit it could make things more awkward.

Of course, there are times when a simple "I'm sorry" doesn't feel like enough. If you need to give a more in-depth apology, be specific. Instead of a vague "Sorry I was being weird," try "I'm sorry I snapped at you earlier. I had a bad day and shouldn't have taken it out on you." Owning your mistake shows sincerity.

Sometimes, even with the best intentions, you can't fix everything. Maybe you deeply offended someone, or your anxiety caused you to act in a way you truly regret. Don't beat yourself up — it happens to everyone! Focus on giving a longer, more heartfelt apology and genuinely making amends if possible. Showing you're trying goes a long way.

Cut yourself some slack! We all say and do awkward things sometimes. Trying to fix every little blip will only make you more self-conscious. Focus on those situations where a sincere apology or quick clarification can smooth things over. Let the minor stuff fade, and remember, most people are far more focused on their own awkward moments than obsessing over yours!

Sometimes, owning your mistakes or clearing the air takes serious guts. That's the kind of confidence that shines way brighter than fake perfection. Speaking of faking it...how do you pull off that "totally chill" vibe when you're freaking out on the inside? That's next!

Emily normally avoided gossip, but one day she slipped up, overhearing part of a conversation and repeating what she thought she'd heard about another girl, Sarah. It turned out to be false, and word got back. Emily felt horrible and immediately apologized to Sarah: "I'm so sorry...I gossiped about you and that was wrong." Sarah was still upset, but appreciated the apology. Emily also talked to the friends she'd repeated the rumor to, setting the record straight to prevent it from spreading further. It was a hard lesson, but it taught her the importance of owning her mistakes and making amends.

## EXERCISE 17: THE APOLOGY REWRITE

✓ Challenge: We've all been there – you mess up, realize you've hurt someone, and the words "I'm sorry" just tumble out of your mouth. But sometimes, a generic apology doesn't cut it. Your task is to transform these vague apologies into specific, sincere ones. Remember, a good apology shows you understand why you messed up and that you genuinely care about the other person's feelings.

✓ Instructions:

1. Get Specific: What exactly are you apologizing for? Instead of "being weird," did you snap at someone, interrupt them, or make a rude comment?

2. Acknowledge Impact: How might your actions have made the other person feel?

3. Show You Get It: Why was your behavior wrong or hurtful?

✓ Example:
- Original: "Sorry if I offended you."
- Rewrite: "I'm sorry I made that insensitive joke earlier. I didn't realize how hurtful it was, and I won't do it again."

| Half-baked | Heartfelt Fix |
|---|---|
| I was just kidding around. | |
| Sorry I was being weird. | |
| My bad, I guess. | |
| Sorry, I messed up. | |
| Whatever, it's not a big deal. | |
| I didn't mean anything by it. | |
| Can we just forget about it? | |

# FAKE IT TILL YOU MAKE IT: HOW TO SEEM, CHILL, WHEN YOU'RE NOT

Okay, let's get real. There are going to be times when you walk into a party, a classroom, or any social situation, and your insides are doing a full-on gymnastics routine. Your heart's pounding, your palms are sweaty, and all you want to do is disappear into thin air. But guess what? There's a way to pull off that "totally relaxed" vibe even when your anxiety is screaming.

The secret weapon? Faking it. Now, I'm not saying you have to be totally dishonest. But there's a big difference between being overwhelmed by anxiety and letting that anxiety control how you act. Think of it like wearing invisible armor – you can still feel a bit shaky on the inside, but on the outside, you project calm and confidence.

Here's your action plan for those "fake it" moments:
- **Body Language Boss**: Stand tall, make eye contact (even if it's briefly), and try to relax your facial muscles. Even if your insides are churning, a confident posture sends a powerful message to your brain (and everyone else).

- **Slow Your Roll:** Anxiety makes you want to rush – rush your words, rush your movements. Consciously slow down your speech and actions just a bit. It tricks your brain into feeling calmer.
- **Focus Outward:** Instead of obsessing over how nervous you are, put your attention on the conversation or the activity around you. Be genuinely curious, ask questions...it shifts the spotlight off yourself (and gives you a breather).
- **The Power Pause:** Feeling a wave of panic rising? Take a mini-break. Excuse yourself to the bathroom, pretend to check your phone, or find a reason to step away for a minute. A few deep breaths can completely reset your system.

Will you feel totally zen instantly? Probably not. But here's the thing about faking it: the more you practice these techniques, the less you'll actually have to fake it. Each time you face a nerve-wracking situation and make it through, your real confidence grows a little bit stronger.

It's important to remember that everyone experiences those "fake it" moments at times. The people who seem the most at ease? They've just gotten really good at managing those anxious feelings, not erasing them completely.

So, next time your anxiety threatens to take over, remember: you've got the tools to project that chill vibe, even when you're secretly freaking out. Of course, there are times when even the best fake-chill vibes crumble. If the conversation takes a nosedive, it's not the end of the world. Mastering the art of the smooth subject change can save the day! ...That's the next skill on our list!

## IN ACTION: STAGE FRIGHT SHOWDOWN

Michael dreaded public speaking – the shaky voice, the sweaty palms, the whole ordeal. But this time, he decided to try the "fake it" approach. He practiced a confident power pose in the mirror, took deep breaths on the bus, and reminded himself, "You've got this." It was still difficult, but he made eye contact, slowed his speech, and focused on the presentation, not his terror. The trembling didn't disappear, but he got through it and even earned some nods of approval. He realized, acting calm helped him feel calmer.

## EXERCISE 18: THE CONFIDENCE MIRROR

✓ Challenge: Think of this as a dress rehearsal for real-life social situations. Standing in front of a mirror lets you see yourself as others do, and experiment with how to project your most awesome self. The point isn't to become someone you're not.

It's about discovering the confident, capable person who's already within you and letting them shine through!

✓ Instructions:

1. Find Your Space: Choose a private spot where you won't be interrupted. A full-length mirror is ideal.
2. Power Poses: Start with your body. Try these confident postures:
   - "The Superhero": Stand tall, feet shoulder-width apart, hands on hips, chin slightly lifted.
   - "The Chill Observer": Lean against a wall, arms relaxed (not crossed!), ankles slightly crossed for a casual vibe.
3. Facetime: Practice different expressions:
   - A genuine smile (not a cheesy grin). Notice how it lifts your whole face.
   - Relaxed eyebrows and a steady gaze. Avoid staring but practice making eye contact with your reflection.
4. Talk the Talk: Here's where it may feel silly, but trust the process! Out loud, try saying things like:
   - "I've got this."
   - "I'm excited to learn new things."
5. Level Up: Once you're comfortable with the basics, try practicing scenarios:
   - Introducing yourself to someone new.
   - Asking a question in class or similar

✓ Tips:

- **Start Short:** Even a few minutes makes a difference. Build up your practice time gradually.
- **Music Helps:** Put on an upbeat song to boost your mood and energy.
- **Laugh It Off:** It's okay if you feel awkward at first. That's part of the process!

# SMOOTH CHANGE OF SUBJECT: SUBTLY REDIRECTING THE CONVO

Picture this: You finally muster up the courage to join the group chat, and – wham! – the convo takes a nosedive into something that makes you want to crawl under a rock. Politics, drama, that super embarrassing thing you wish never happened – whatever it is, your anxiety is screaming.

Don't panic, you've got this! It's time to channel your inner conversation ninja. You're not going to shut down the whole chat, just gently guide it to a place where you feel more chill.

Your Convo Switcharoo Tools:

- **The "That Reminds Me" Pivot:** This one's a classic. Someone mentions a band – boom! Time to share about that awesome concert you went to. New topic unlocked!
- **The Question Bounce:** Feeling flustered? Ask the group a question instead. "Anyone got fun weekend plans?" or "What's everyone's thoughts on [new series/song/whatever]?" gets the ball rolling in a different direction.
- **Compliment Power:** Not everyone's into this, but a genuine "Love those shoes!" can buy you a breather to regroup and shift the topic.
- **Direct but Polite:** "Hey, I really appreciate you wanting to talk about [difficult topic], but I'm honestly not feeling up to it right now. How about we talk about [lighter subject] instead?"
- **Find Common Ground:** Overhearing someone mention a hobby you're into: "Wait, did you say you play [that game]? I love it! What's your favorite character/strategy/etc.?"

- **Relate to Personal Experience.** Someone mentions struggling with a class: "Ugh, I totally get that. [Specific subject] is kicking my butt too. Any study tips?"
- **Humorous Escape.** When the topic gets too deep: "All right, my brain is officially overloaded. Let's talk about something ridiculous, like if animals had jobs, what would they be?"

Let's be real, sometimes there's just no saving it. The chat's a dumpster fire, someone's being a total troll... you are 100% allowed to bail. Hit 'em with the classic "Homework emergency!" excuse, or just ghost the chat. Self-care comes first! The more you practice these ninja moves, the easier it gets. The key is finding ways to steer the chat toward things that don't leave you feeling stressed. Own those convos – it's the ultimate flex!

But let's be honest – sometimes the convo isn't the problem, it's everything ELSE swirling around in your head. Time to tackle those school stress triggers so you can actually chill when those convos do happen.

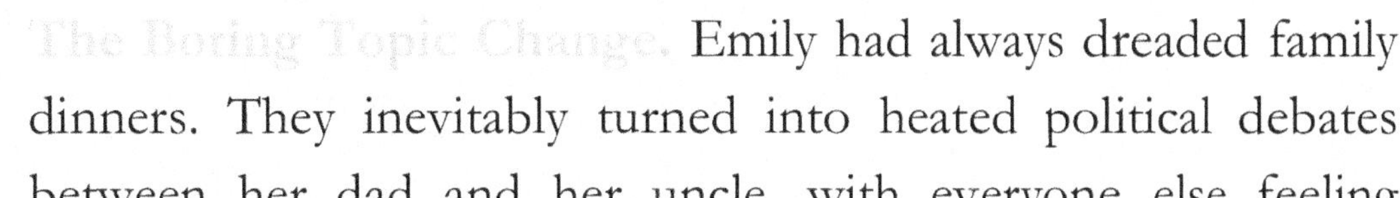

✓ **The Boring Topic Change.** Emily had always dreaded family dinners. They inevitably turned into heated political debates between her dad and her uncle, with everyone else feeling awkward and uninvolved. This time, she was determined not to let it ruin her evening. As soon as her uncle started launching into his usual rant, Emily was ready. She casually mentioned, "Speaking of crazy energy, did you guys hear that I got a new puppy? It's a total tornado of fur!" Her cousin immediately piped up, wanting to see pictures and share stories about her dog. Before long, the whole table was laughing about puppy antics, completely forgetting about politics.

*The Awkward Compliment Save.* Michael was ready to disappear when the conversation at his lunch table turned to his epic faceplant during gym class. He could feel his face flushing as everyone started rehashing the moment in hilarious detail. Desperate to change the subject, he noticed the cool new sneakers on the girl sitting across from him. "Whoa, I love your kicks!" he blurted out. "Where'd you get those?" Thankfully, she was a sneakerhead and happily launched into a discussion about her favorite brands and upcoming releases. Michael was able to relax and even join in, successfully diverting attention from his embarrassing moment.

Part 4:

# BEYOND THE WORRY: LEVEL UP YOUR LIFE

# INSIDE THIS PART

Ever feel like you have a mean little critic living in your head? It tells you you're not smart enough, that everyone secretly thinks you're a loser, and that you're going to mess everything up. Seriously, who needs that kind of negativity? Time to kick that bully to the curb! This section is all about transforming your mindset and ditching that self-doubt for good.

We're about to dive into ACT (Acceptance and Commitment Therapy). It's a different way of dealing with those harsh thoughts and feelings, so they don't control you anymore. Think of it like learning secret mind-control tricks to shut down that inner critic and focus on what truly matters. Get ready to discover your inner badass and start living life your way!

# CHAPTER 10:

# SELF-CARE FTW: KEEPING YOUR CHILL GAME STRONG

Think of self-care as the ultimate mental health power-up. It's NOT about bubble baths and scented candles (though those can be nice!). It's about finding what TRULY helps you destress and recharge your batteries when anxiety makes life feel overwhelming.

In this chapter, we're going to ditch the one-size-fits-all self-care advice and get serious about what works for YOU. You'll figure out your personal stress-busters, how to navigate schoolwork without freaking out, and when to put your phone down because social media is making things worse. Get ready to discover the chill routine that keeps your anxiety in check and lets you live your life on your own terms!

# RECHARGE: FINDING THE THINGS THAT DESTRESS YOU

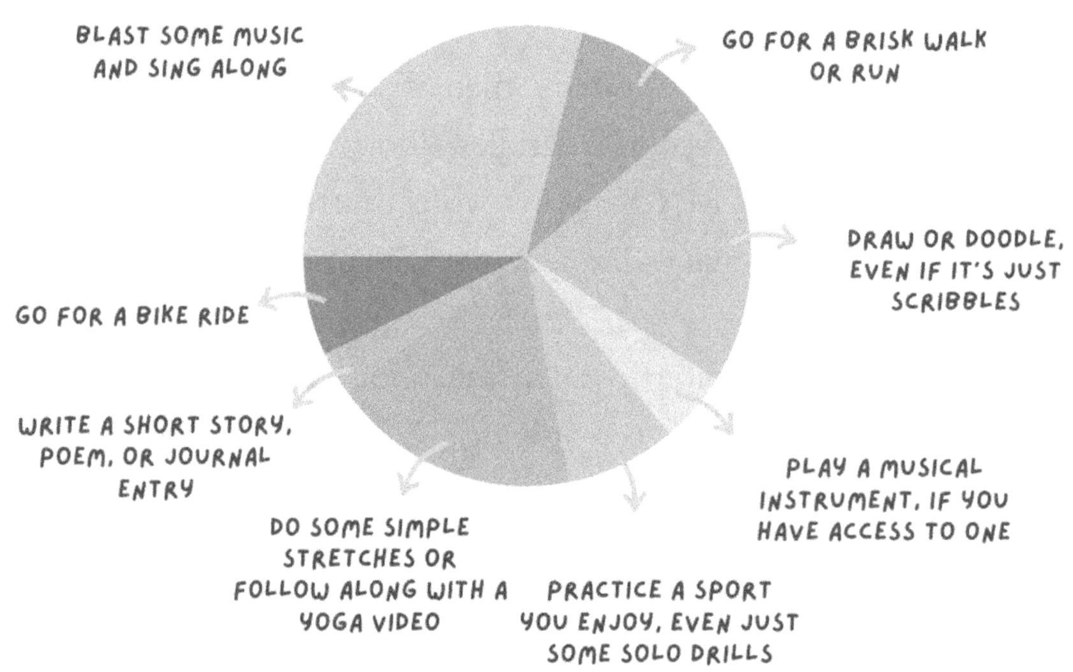


Imagine your phone at 5% battery – that flashing warning, the laggy apps, it's basically useless. That's your brain after a long day of school, social overload, and dealing with anxiety on top of it all. Trying to power through is a recipe for a full-on meltdown. That's where recharging comes in.

Forget about fancy spa days (unless that's your thing, no judgment here!). This is about finding what reboots your brain. If blasting music and having a solo dance party does the trick – awesome! Maybe you need the total opposite – chilling under a blanket with a favorite book or cuddling your pet. The coolest part is, your recharge zone is totally up to you.

Experiment with it! Get creative with drawing or writing, build something, get outside, or find the dumbest YouTube videos ever for a guaranteed laugh. It's about finding those things that shift your brain from "freak-out mode" to "I got this". The more drained you are, the stronger your anxiety gets. But imagine facing all that school stress after a good recharge session? Still tough, but you're way better equipped to handle it.

Don't let anyone tell you that needing downtime is lazy. Taking care of your mental health makes you a total boss. Schedule those recharge moments, even if it's just 15 minutes. You wouldn't let your phone die completely, so why do it to your brain?

Because let's face it, sometimes school feels like it was designed to make you lose your cool. But here's the thing, you're not alone. I'm about to show you how to handle those anxiety-fueled school freakouts, one crazy deadline and awkward group project at a time.

## PARENT TIP: CALMING HOME ENVIRONMENT

✓ Less Chaos, More Chill: Can you reduce clutter, turn down noisy electronics, or create a designated "zen zone" for de-stressing? A calmer environment benefits everyone.

✓ Soothing Rituals: Simple things like a family walk after dinner, a quiet playlist, or turning off screens an hour before bed can signal relaxation time.

✓ Parent Self-Care Matters Too: Modeling your own stress-reducing habits (taking breaks, exercise, etc.) shows teens the importance of taking care of themselves

## IN ACTION: THE HOMEWORK HERO

✓ Emily used to get major anxiety before tests. Her heart would pound, her palms would sweat, and her mind would race. She found it almost impossible to concentrate, and her grades were suffering. Desperate for a change, Emily talked to her school counselor who suggested practicing relaxation techniques. Now, she spends 15 minutes before any test doing deep breathing exercises and listening to her favorite upbeat playlist. She finds this helps calm her nerves and allows her to focus more clearly, resulting in a huge boost in her test scores and overall confidence.

# HANDLING SCHOOL STRESS: WHEN ANXIETY MAKES IT WORSE

Okay, let's be real. School is already a pressure cooker of deadlines, tests, and that awkward shuffle of trying to find your place socially. Toss in some anxiety, and bam! You're looking at a recipe for a full-blown meltdown. It's like your brain gets stuck in freak-out mode, and even the smallest things feel HUGE.

But here's the secret weapon: understanding how stress fuels your anxiety, and vice-versa, is the first step to taking back control. Think of them as those annoying cartoon villains that become stronger when they team up.

Picture this: You've got a big presentation coming up. If you have social anxiety, just the thought of it alone can send your heart racing. Suddenly, studying is impossible because all you can focus on is messing up in front of everyone. This stress then stokes the fire of your anxiety, making those scary scenarios seem even more likely. Now the presentation feels downright impossible! And so the cycle begins – more stress, more anxiety, and a whole lot of dread.

So, how do we break it? By building your own anxiety-busting toolkit, starting with something called "recharge". These are activities that help reset your brain, shifting it from overwhelmed to ready to rumble (or at least ready to tolerate that presentation).

Finding your perfect recharge zone takes some experimenting. Maybe it's blasting music while you do chores, sketching whatever crazy thing pops into your head, or getting lost in a video game. Remember, there's no right or wrong way to recharge – it's about what works for YOU.

Think of those recharge moments as armor. Can you still get stressed at school? Of course! But with consistent practice, you'll start noticing a shift. Imagine facing that presentation after a 15-minute walk outside or a quick journaling session to get the worries out of your head. Tough? Absolutely. But suddenly, you might feel more grounded and capable.

Taking those recharge breaks isn't laziness; it's a strategic move for your mental health. School is designed to push you, and the pressure is real. But remember, you don't have to let stress and anxiety win every time.

You can build your resilience so that even on the most difficult days, you can remind yourself, "This sucks right now, but I've got this."

So yeah, school can be a total stress-fest, especially with anxiety breathing down your neck. But remember, you've got the power to change how you handle it. Now, let's be real, social media can be a whole other beast…

IN ACTION: RECHARGE AND CONQUER

Anna dreaded presentations. The mix of social anxiety and pressure made them unbearable. She'd prep, but the worry spiral would take over, leaving her sleepless and convinced of disaster. After a particularly rough presentation, Anna knew she had to try something different. She'd heard about "recharge" breaks, and out of desperation, took a short walk before her next presentation. Focusing on the fresh air calmed her racing thoughts, even sparking some new ideas. While still nervous, the panic was gone. She used some calming breathing techniques before starting, and though there were stumbles, she made it through. Anna realized recharge time wasn't wasted – it was vital for keeping her anxiety from winning. It was a struggle, but she now had tools to break the stress-anxiety cycle.

# WHEN SOCIAL MEDIA MAKES IT WORSE

## DON'T LET 'LIKES' DICTATE YOUR WORTH.

School can be a mega-dose of stress, especially when you're battling anxiety. But here's the thing – sometimes, the moment you escape those hallways, the pressure isn't really gone. It's just waiting for you on your phone.

Think about it: you get home, drop your backpack, and instinctively reach for your phone to scroll. What should be a break often becomes a weird mix of FOMO (remember, Fear Of Missing Out?), comparison, and maybe a touch of doom-scrolling (you know, when you get sucked into a rabbit hole of bad news).

This is where it gets especially tricky if you have anxiety, particularly social anxiety. Social media is designed to be, well, social. You're seeing what other people are up to – the parties, the hangouts, the seemingly perfect filtered lives. Even if you logically know nobody's life is that flawless, your anxious brain doesn't always listen to logic. It starts whispering, "What's wrong with me? Why don't I have that?"

Maybe you start obsessing about how many likes you get, if that person responded to your message, or if that comment was secretly making fun of you. Suddenly, social media makes your brain spin even faster instead of giving you that recharge you were hoping for. And who feels good overthinking every post? Definitely not you.

But here's the deal (therapist talk here): awareness is everything. Once you realize that social media can be a legit anxiety trigger, you can build some defenses against it. It won't suddenly become your favorite place, and there'll be days where logging off is the absolute best self-care. But you can learn how to use it more mindfully, instead of it using you.

So, how do we tackle this? Let's dive into some strategies, tools, and maybe a good dose of healthy skepticism for those picture-perfect posts…No need to ditch your phone entirely, but it's about making smarter choices. Here's your starter kit:

- **The Unfollow Button:** It's Your Friend. Anyone who consistently drags you down, makes you feel bad about yourself or triggers your comparison spiral? Unfollow! It's not mean, it's self-preservation. Make your feed a more positive space.

- **Mute Those Notifications.** Those constant pings and buzzes? They hijack your brain, making it difficult to focus. Turn off most notifications. Check your apps on your schedule, not theirs.
- **Time Limits to the Rescue.** Mindless scrolling is a major time-suck, leaving you feeling drained instead of entertained. Most phones have built-in app timers. Set limits, and when the time's up, do something else.
- **Reality Check Challenge.** Next time you see a "perfect" post, play a little game. Ask yourself: "What's not in this picture?" The 20 failed attempts, the argument they had earlier, the messy room just outside the frame...
- **Break Up with the Comparison Trap.** This one takes practice, but it's a game-changer. Remember, everyone's journey is different. Focus on your progress, and celebrate your wins (big or small). Compare yourself to...yourself a month ago. Are you kinder to yourself now? Handling a tough situation better? That's growth!

Sometimes, you do want to see what your friends are up to. Before you open your apps, do this:

- **Body Check-In:** How are you feeling? Any tightness, racing heart, or shallow breathing? Those are clues you might be a bit anxious already.
- **Why Now?:** Are you truly bored, or are you procrastinating, feeling lonely, or avoiding something?

- **Tech Tools To The Rescue:**
    - ○ **"News Feed Eradicator":** This extension hides that endless scroll of posts on Facebook and Instagram, so you focus on specific friends instead.
    - ○ **StayFocusd (Chrome extension):** This lets you block or limit time on distracting websites. Perfect for avoiding those rabbit holes when you're supposed to be studying.
    - ○ **Forest (App):** A playful way to stay focused. Plant a virtual tree – if you leave the app, your tree dies! Earns you points to plant real trees.
    - ○ **Grayscale Mode:** Turn your phone's display black and white. Those colorful app icons suddenly lose their appeal.
    - ○ **App Timers:** Set strict limits for how long to use certain apps to break the mindless scrolling habit.
- **Bonus Tip:** If it all feels too much, taking a complete break from social media is the ultimate reset. A day, a weekend...it might feel weird at first, but you could be surprised how freeing it is.

And look, even with the best strategies, there'll be moments when you scroll into a full-blown tailspin. It's normal, and we'll talk about how to handle those "Oops, I spiraled" moments next.

## EXERCISE 19: SOCIAL MEDIA AUDIT 

✓ The Time Tracker Challenge: Ready to take charge of your social media habits? For the next three days, let's uncover how much time you're spending scrolling. You can use a simple notebook or your phone's built-in screen time tracker. No judgment here - this isn't about guilt, it's about empowerment! Think of it like a detective mission: gather the data on those quick checks between classes, mindless scrolling sessions, and all those minutes that add up. The more honest you are, the better equipped you'll be to make those awesome changes. This exercise is your key to unlocking more time for activities that truly energize and inspire you. Let's get started!

✓ Step 2: Analyze the Results. After three days, look at your totals. Are you surprised? Maybe a little shocked? Don't worry, you're not alone! Most of us spend way more time scrolling than we realize.

✓ Step 3: Imagine the Possibilities. Now, here's the fun part. Brainstorm: What ELSE could you do with that time? Here are some ideas to get you started:

- Get creative: Draw, write, play an instrument, try a new recipe

- **Get learning:** Read a book, pick up a skill online, watch a documentary
- **Get connected:** Call a friend you haven't talked to in a while, and spend time in person with your people.
- **Get moving:** Walk, dance, try a new sport, explore your neighborhood

# CHAPTER 11:

# OOPS, I SPIRALED: HANDLING SETBACKS WITHOUT FREAKING OUT

Setbacks happen. Sometimes you have a bad day, an awkward encounter triggers old fears, or you totally lose your chill over something that seems minor. It sucks, but it's completely normal, especially when you're dealing with anxiety!

This chapter is about damage control when those spirals hit. We'll cover how to calm yourself down in the moment, how to get back on track without beating yourself up, and the importance of celebrating those small wins (because progress isn't always a straight line). Think of this as your emergency recovery kit for those moments when anxiety tries to knock you down. You got this!

# GOALS AND WINS: CELEBRATING THE SMALL STUFF

Okay, let's get real: battling anxiety can feel like you're climbing a mountain made of quicksand (major struggle!). Some days, just getting through feels like a win in itself. But here's the thing: those "just getting through" days are packed with tiny victories you might be missing.

Picture this: You've got a big presentation that has you freaking out. Maybe you usually bail on practicing because the fear feels crushing. But this time, you manage to force yourself to open your notes for 10 minutes.

Or during the presentation, even though you're anxious, you make eye contact with the audience, something you never would have done before. Those are wins! Yeah, they might not feel like fireworks-in-your-brain wins, but they prove you're getting stronger. Think of it like this: you don't get ripped after one workout, right? It takes consistent effort and celebrating those gains along the way.

Why bother with the small stuff? A few reasons:

- **Motivation Fuel:** When you're feeling down, reminding yourself "Hey, I actually rocked that tough conversation yesterday" keeps you going.
- **Spotting Patterns:** Keeping track of your wins (even just quick notes on your phone) helps you see what makes you feel good and capable.
- **Fighting the Negativity Bias:** Let's face it, our brains can be drama queens, fixating on what went wrong. Celebrating wins actively retrains your focus.

So, how do we make this a habit? It's not about being fake-happy, it's about shifting your attention. Try this:

- **End of Day Win-Scan:** Before bed, ask yourself, "What's one thing I did today, however small, that took courage or was a step outside my comfort zone?"
- **Make a "Win Jar":** Got a jar and some scrap paper? Jot down your wins and drop them in. Feeling blah? Pull a few and give them a re-read.

Look, progress isn't a straight line (more on that next chapter!). But celebrating those small wins reminds you that you're on an upward path, even if it feels slow sometimes. And recognizing how far you've come? Now THAT's definitely worth celebrating.

And the truth is, even the strongest of us have those "taking a few steps backward" days. That's okay, it happens, and it doesn't undo your progress. Let's talk about how to handle those moments without totally losing it.

## IN ACTION: THE PROGRESS TRACKER

Michael felt trapped in a loop with his social anxiety. He longed to connect with his classmates, but fear always held him back. Even on the days he forced himself to try, it felt like he just embarrassed himself, making him feel hopeless. Then, a therapist suggested a "win jar". Each time Michael faced a social fear, no matter how tiny, he'd write it down and add it to the jar – making eye contact, asking a question in class, or even just attending a school event he'd usually avoid. The jar filled slowly at first, but Michael was surprised at how his wins accumulated. Rereading them gave him a much-needed sense of accomplishment. More importantly, it shifted his mindset. Instead of obsessing over the awkward moments, he began to see his gradual progress, proving to himself that he was becoming braver, one small step at a time.

## PARENT TIP: REACTING SUPPORTIVELY 

✓ Acknowledge the Feels: Even when their worries seem overblown, let them know their emotions are valid ("This feels super hard right now."). This builds trust.

✓ Avoid Minimizing: Phrases like "Don't worry about it" or "It's not a big deal" can make them feel rejected. Focus on what they CAN control: "What might help you calm down right now?"

✓ Learning from It: Once they're less overwhelmed, you can gently explore: "What do you think triggered that spiral?", "Is there anything you'd do differently next time?"

# TWO STEPS FORWARD, ONE STEP BACK – STILL PROGRESS!



Picture this: You've been crushing it with your anxiety-busting techniques. Maybe you finally spoke up in that class where you usually hide, or you managed to chill during a presentation instead of totally freaking out. You're on top of the world...until you have one of those days. You know the ones – where it feels like all your progress vanishes, and anxiety comes roaring back. It's enough to make you want to hide under the covers forever.

But here's the deal (and something those cheesy motivational posters forget): Progress rarely goes in a straight line. It's more like a crazy hiking trail – some uphill struggles, some easier stretches, and the occasional slip where you land on your butt. Those slip-ups? Totally normal, and they don't erase how far you've come.

Think of it like building muscle. You don't get ripped overnight, right? Some days you crush those weights. On other days, your arms feel like noodles. But even on the noodle-arm days, you're getting stronger. Handling anxiety is the same. The more you practice your skills, the more resilient you become – even when it feels like you're back to square one.

So how do we handle those setbacks without losing it? Here's the plan:

- Don't let one bad day wreck you. Everyone messes up sometimes. Instead of spiraling into "I suck, this is hopeless" mode, remind yourself of a recent win. You handled that tough situation way better than you would have before, didn't you?
- Zoom out for the big picture. It's easy to get obsessed with the moment. Try to see the longer journey. Journaling your wins (even tiny ones) helps with this.
- Cut yourself some slack. Would you talk to a friend struggling the way you talk to yourself? Be your own hype person, remember, progress takes time.

The awesome thing is, even when it feels like a step backward, you're actually learning how to handle those tough moments. That in itself is a major win. So, dust yourself off, remember all those times you've rocked it, and keep going. Because even wobbly steps still count!

Remember, detours and rough patches are part of the journey. Just keep moving in the general direction of progress, and those setbacks will start to feel smaller. Now, let's get into your HEADSPACE and upgrade that inner voice to be your biggest supporter, not your worst enemy.

## IN ACTION: THE SOCIAL SETBACK SURVIVOR

Emily always dreamed of being that girl who could walk into a party and effortlessly chat with everyone. But her social anxiety made that feel impossible. This time, she decided to try. It was hard, way harder than she expected. Halfway through, that familiar panicky feeling started rising. She had to duck into the bathroom to calm down and almost bailed completely. But then, Emily remembered why she came: to push herself. Taking a few deep breaths, she went back out. Even though she ended up leaving early, it still felt like a win. She faced her fear, had a few good conversations, and proved to herself that she could handle it, even when it wasn't perfect.

## EXERCISE 20: SETBACK REFRAME CHALLENGE 

✓ Challenge: Setbacks are an inevitable part of life, especially when you're battling anxiety. They can feel totally crummy in the moment. But here's the thing: even within those setbacks, there's usually a sliver of something positive if you look for it. This isn't about pretending the bad stuff didn't happen, it's about training your brain to spot the growth alongside the struggle. Setbacks are going to happen. But how you view them makes a huge difference. The reframe challenge helps you build that resilience muscle over time. The next time you face a setback, it'll feel a little less daunting because you'll know you can find the hidden wins, even on the toughest days. Here's how it works:

✓ Step 1: Think of a recent setback. Big or small, choose a situation where you felt like anxiety got the best of you. Maybe you froze up during a presentation, avoided something you wanted to do, or had a major meltdown over something minor.

✓ Step 2: Vent It Out (Optional). If it helps, jot down all the negative thoughts and feelings you had in the moment. Getting it out of your system can make it easier to approach the situation more calmly.

✓ Step 3: The Reframe Hunt. Now, try to find even the tiniest win or positive within the experience. Here are some ways to reframe:

- The "I Tried" Win: Did you push yourself out of your comfort zone, even if the outcome wasn't ideal?
- The "I Endured" Win: Did you make it through something that felt incredibly difficult in the moment?
- The "Learning Moment" Win: Did you realize something about how your anxiety works, or a trigger you hadn't noticed before? Can you use this knowledge to make another choice next time?

✓ Step 4: Write it Down. Record your setback and your reframed win. It doesn't have to be fancy – a note on your phone works. Revisiting these later is a great way to remind yourself of your progress.

Part 5:

MINDSET MAKEOVER: CRUSH THE SELF-DOUBT MONSTER

# INSIDE THIS PART

Ever feel like you have a mean little critic living in your head? It tells you you're not smart enough, that everyone secretly thinks you're a loser, and that you're going to mess everything up. Seriously, who needs that kind of negativity? Time to kick that bully to the curb! This section is all about transforming your mindset and ditching that self-doubt for good.

We're about to dive into ACT (Acceptance and Commitment Therapy). It's a different way of dealing with those harsh thoughts and feelings, so they don't control you anymore. Think of it like learning secret mind-control tricks to shut down that inner critic and focus on what truly matters. Get ready to discover your inner badass and start living life your way!

# CHAPTER 12:

## INTRO TO ACT: TOOLS FOR THE TOUGH STUFF

Sometimes it feels like your brain is on a negativity loop, and no matter how hard you try, you can't shut those worries down. CBT is great for fighting back, but what if you could find a way to chill with those tough thoughts instead? That's where ACT comes in!

ACT (Acceptance and Commitment Therapy) is about learning to roll with those difficult thoughts and feelings instead of getting stuck in a battle with them. You'll discover why trying to be happy 24/7 can actually make things worse, how to focus on what REALLY matters to you, and why doing what's important – even when it's scary – is how you start living your best life. Think of it as a new set of mental flexibility skills for when your brain gets in its own way.

# WHAT THE HECK IS ACT?: IT'S KINDA DIFFERENT... (A NEW APPROACH TO HANDLING TOUGH THOUGHTS)

Okay, you've already known about CBT (Cognitive Behavioral Therapy). It's all about changing those negative thought patterns that fuel anxiety, right? Well, ACT (Acceptance and Commitment Therapy) is like CBT's slightly rebellious cousin. It still has solid science behind it, but it tackles anxiety from a different angle.

Here's the thing: sometimes, trying to fight or change your anxious thoughts can backfire. The more you obsess over how awful they are, the more powerful they seem. That's where ACT comes in.

Think of your mind like a super annoying pop-up ad. You know those ones that take over your whole screen, with the tiny "X" to close it? The more you fight the pop-up, the more frustrating it becomes. ACT is like teaching you to take a step back and say, "Okay, I see you over there, annoying ad. I'm not going to click on you, but I'm also not going to waste all my energy fighting you."

So, how does ACT actually work? A few key ideas:

- **Acceptance (But Like, Not in a Defeated Way):** This is about acknowledging those anxious thoughts and feelings without getting all tangled up in them. It doesn't mean you agree with them, or like them – just that they're there for now.
- **Mindfulness:** ACT uses mindfulness techniques to help you observe your thoughts more calmly, almost like they're clouds drifting by instead of a thunderstorm inside your head.
- **Values:** What truly matters to you in life? ACT helps you connect with your core values (kindness, creativity, friendship, etc.) and use those as your compass, even when anxiety tries to steer you off course.
- **Committed Action:** This is about taking steps towards what matters to you, anxiety and all. Instead of waiting to feel perfectly "ready", ACT is about brave, imperfect action.

Okay, some of these might sound a bit weird compared to other stuff you've already tried. But trust me, ACT can be a game-changer, especially if you're tired of wrestling with your own brain. Ready to dive deeper into how this actually works in real life? Let's explore the first key idea: The Flexibility Factor.

IN ACTION: THE CONTROL STRUGGLE

Anna used to avoid anything that triggered her social anxiety. The thought of going to a party would send her into a spiral — "I'm going to say something embarrassing," "Everyone will notice how awkward I am," etc. She'd either cancel at the last minute or spend the whole time feeling miserable. Lately, she's been trying some ACT techniques. Now, instead of wrestling with those anxious thoughts, she acknowledges them, then reminds herself: "Hey, those are just my anxiety brain doing its thing. They don't control me. I can still go to the party and have a good time, even if I feel a little nervous at first." This doesn't make the anxiety vanish, but it stops her from getting sucked into the old panic cycle.

**PARENT TIP: THE POWER OF VALIDATION**

- ✓ Acknowledge the Feels: Even when their worries seem overblown, let them know their emotions are valid ("This feels super hard right now."). This builds trust, so they're more receptive to the next step...

- ✓ The ACT Twist: Follow up with, "Feeling anxious doesn't mean there's anything wrong with you. And there ARE things we can do to help you cope." This emphasizes action over getting stuck in the negativity.

- ✓ Choices, Not Cures: Remind them, "ACT isn't about making the anxiety disappear, it's about learning to live a full life even when anxiety shows up." This fosters a sense of control.

# THE FLEXIBILITY FACTOR: WHY ACT HELPS YOU ROLL WITH THE PUNCHES

Remember that pop-up ad analogy? Where you learn to stop fighting it and just let it be there? That's the first step toward what ACT calls psychological flexibility.

Think of it like this: Mental flexibility is like being made of rubber instead of stiff wood. When life throws a curveball (and trust me, it will), you can bend and adapt instead of snapping under pressure.

Face it, so many teens get stuck in the perfection trap — if it's not perfect, it's a failure, right? A bad grade, an awkward comment, a plan gone wrong...and boom, full-on meltdown. ACT helps you break free of this in a few ways:

- **Letting Go of the Struggle:** Fighting those anxious thoughts often backfires. ACT teaches you to acknowledge them without letting them hijack your whole day.
- **Embracing the "And":** Before, it might have been "I'm anxious AND I can't do this." ACT helps you shift to "I'm anxious AND I'm going to try anyway." That little word makes a huge difference!
- **Focusing on What You CAN Control:** You can't control every thought or feeling. But you CAN control your actions, even when it's scary.

Let's make this real. Imagine you're dreading a class presentation. Old-school anxiety advice is like "Just think positive!" ACT is more realistic. You practice noticing those anxious thoughts ("I'm going to bomb this").

You do some calming techniques, and then remind yourself: "I prepared, I can handle a little discomfort, and I'm doing this because speaking up is important to me." It won't make the anxiety vanish, but it puts YOU back in the driver's seat.

ACT flexibility helps you roll with the punches of life instead of getting knocked out by them. It's what lets you take those brave, imperfect steps toward what matters to you, even when your anxious brain is freaking out. With this kind of flexibility, you're less likely to get bogged down by setbacks or self-doubt. But how do you know which direction to "bend" in, especially when anxiety tries to throw you off course? That's where your values come in – like your own personal North Star.

## EXERCISE 24: THE FLEXIBILITY SCALE

✓ Challenge: How mentally flexible do you feel? This quick exercise will give you a better sense of where you're already rocking it, and where you might need a little extra bendiness. This exercise isn't about being perfect. It's about noticing your patterns. The more aware you are of where you tend to get stuck, the easier it is to start building that mental flexibility muscle!

✓ Instructions: Read each situation below. On a scale of 1-5, rate how flexible you think you'd handle it (1 = "Total meltdown", 5 = "I can roll with this").

| Situation | Rate |
| --- | --- |
| You get a bad grade on a test you studied hard for. | |
| Your friend cancels plans at the last minute. | |
| You have to give a presentation and technology fails at the worst moment. | |
| Someone makes a rude comment about something you're passionate about. | |
| A big, unexpected change happens in your life (a move, a family situation, etc.) | |

✓ Reflect:

- Where did you score the highest? Lowest? Any surprises?
- Are there certain types of situations that are harder to handle flexibly?
- Choose ONE situation where you want to boost your flexibility.

# VALUES VS. GOALS: FINDING YOUR INTERNAL COMPASS

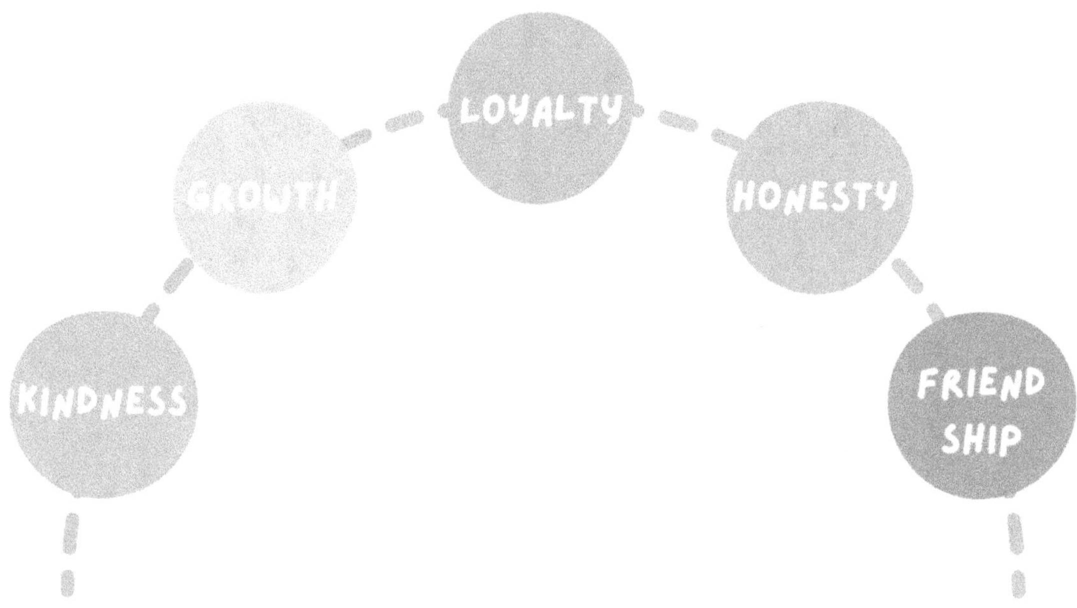


Okay, we've talked about flexibility – bending instead of breaking under pressure. But what if you're so caught up in the storm of anxiety that you don't even know which direction to bend in? That's where values come in.

Think of your values as your personal North Star. They're the things that are deeply important to you, the kind of person you want to be. Things like kindness, creativity, loyalty, standing up for what's right, etc. Unlike goals, which are often about achievement or external stuff, values are about who you are at your core.

**Here's Why This Matters for Anxiety:**
- **Anxiety is a Master of Distraction:** It gets you obsessed with fears, what-ifs, and beating yourself up. Your values help you reconnect with what truly matters, even when anxiety tries to drown them out.
- **Goals Can Backfire:** If your sense of worth depends on always being perfect (hello, fellow perfectionists!), failing to reach a goal can feel devastating. Values give you a sense of purpose that's less shaky.
- **Decisions Get Easier:** When faced with a choice, ask yourself: Does this action align with my values? If not, it's easier to walk away, no matter how tempting it seems in the moment.

But How Do You Even Find Your Values? There's no single "right" way, but here's a starting point:
- **Think of People You Admire:** What qualities do you respect in them? Those could point to your own values.
- **Recall a High Point:** A time you felt proud of yourself. What made that moment meaningful?
- **Your Anger Can Be a Clue:** What makes you so angry that you want to fight for change? That often reveals a deep-seated value.

Don't get hung up on finding the perfect words. Your values can change over time, this is just about getting clearer on what guides your decisions.

Having that internal compass is key, but it won't magically get you where you want to go. You need committed action – and that's where things get tough. Anxiety will try to trick you, your inner critic will be loud...how do you push through anyway? Time to get strategic.

## IN ACTION: REDEFINING SUCCESS

✓ **The Conflicted Athlete.** Emily lived for basketball. The harder she practiced, the better she played – that's just how it worked. Except lately, something wasn't working. Practices felt like torture, games were filled with dread, and she was snapping at her teammates over tiny mistakes. Deep down, she was terrified of letting everyone down, of failing, of not being the star anymore. Then, her coach suggested something weird – focusing on values like teamwork and enjoying the process instead of obsessing over results. At first, it felt silly. But slowly, Emily remembered why she fell in love with basketball in the first place. She still works hard, but now, there's more joy in the effort itself.

✓ **The Directionless Dreamer.** Michael was always starting things – guitar lessons, that cool coding class, volunteering at the shelter...and then abandoning them a few weeks later. He'd get excited, but then the next shiny thing would catch his eye. "Jack of all trades, master of none," his dad would say, which just made Michael feel like a loser. Lately, he's been thinking about values instead. He realized he thrives on trying new stuff, on learning just for the sake of it. So, is it really a failure if he never becomes an expert? Maybe success looks more like diving into experiences wholeheartedly, even if they're temporary.

# COMMITTED ACTION: DOING WHAT MATTERS, EVEN WHEN IT'S HARD

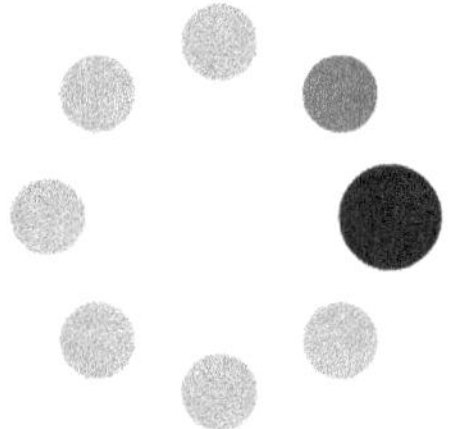

## OVERCOMING FEAR: 85% COMPLETE

Okay, let's face it: anxiety stinks. It can be like this invisible forcefield trying to hold you back from all the things you want to do. Maybe it whispers that you'll fail that test, or you'll make a fool of yourself at the party. Sometimes, the biggest hurdle isn't the test or the party – it's getting yourself to take the first step.

That's where committed action comes in. It's a fancy way of saying "doing what matters to you, even when your brain is screaming at you to run in the opposite direction." It's about facing the stuff that scares you, not because you're suddenly a fearless daredevil, but because there's something deeper inside you that wants to move forward.

Imagine you're in a tug-of-war with your anxiety. Anxiety is that super-strong opponent, trying to pull you backward. Committed action is finding that extra boost of strength and refusing to let go of the rope. It's deciding your values matter more than your fears. Maybe you really want to make friends, but social anxiety makes you want to hide under a rock. Committed action would be taking a tiny step, like saying hi to the person next to you in class or joining a club that seems halfway interesting. Is it scary? Heck yeah! But every time you face that small fear, you become a little stronger.

The thing is, committed action isn't about being some fearless superhero. It's about acknowledging the fear and doing it anyway. You know how in video games you start off weak but get better with practice? It's the same with anxiety. The more you practice those committed actions, the less power your fear has. You're basically upgrading your "brave" skill!

Remember those values we talked about earlier? Figuring out the things that really matter to you is like having a compass when anxiety tries to send you in circles. Committed action is how you take steps in the direction your compass points, even if it's just a tiny step at a time.

Committed action gets hard sometimes. There will be days when anxiety wins a round of that tug-of-war. That's okay! It happens to everyone. The key is not giving up the fight long-term. Get back up, dust yourself off, and remember why you're pushing yourself in the first place. The easy path leads to staying stuck in the same place, but that path paved with committed action, even if it has bumps and weird detours, leads you toward the life you truly want.

Taking action aligned with your values? That's a major power move, even if it doesn't feel that way right now. But guess what? Your anxiety brain isn't the only voice in your head. It's time to unleash your inner champion and drown out that negativity. Let's expose those self-doubt lies for what they are!

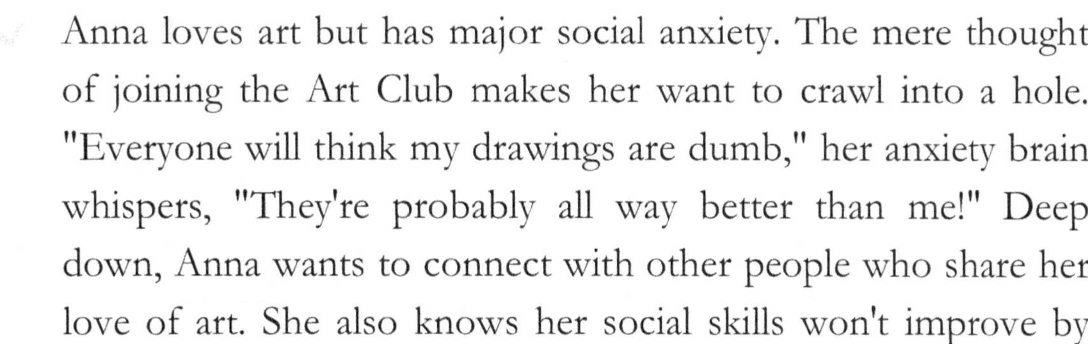


Anna loves art but has major social anxiety. The mere thought of joining the Art Club makes her want to crawl into a hole. "Everyone will think my drawings are dumb," her anxiety brain whispers, "They're probably all way better than me!" Deep down, Anna wants to connect with other people who share her love of art. She also knows her social skills won't improve by hiding. Committed action means taking that first, scary step: "Okay, I'm going to go to one Art Club meeting. Just one, to see what it's like." Anna walks in feeling awkward and exposed. She finds a corner to sketch in, trying to blend into the background. It takes courage, but eventually, she shows her drawing to the person next to her. They actually compliment a cool detail in her artwork! It's not a magical friendship moment, but it's a start. Leaving the meeting, Anna thinks, "That was hard, BUT I survived. Maybe...that's a win."

## EXERCISE 22: SMALL WINS WORKSHEET 

✓ Challenge: This tracker is all about celebrating those moments when you face your anxiety and do the hard stuff. Keep it simple and focus on the wins, no matter how small they may seem.

✓ How to Use It:

1. Today I Did... Describe a committed action you took. It could be:

   ○ "I spoke up in class even though my voice was shaky."

- o "I went to that party for an hour, even though I wanted to hide."
- o "I started studying earlier instead of waiting until the last minute."

2. It Felt... Be honest about the emotions:
- o "Scary, awkward, but also a little bit proud."
- o "Overwhelming, but I calmed myself down enough to finish."
- o "Hard at first, then surprisingly manageable."

3. Proud of Myself Because... Finish this sentence:
- o "I didn't let my fear hold me back completely."
- o "I proved I'm stronger than my anxiety voice."
- o "I took a step towards something I want."

✓ Tips:
- Date Your Entries: So you can track how far you come!
- No Pressure: Some days you won't have an entry, but that's okay.
- Reread and Reflect: Look back at your old entries – those little victories add up!

# CHAPTER 13:

# INNER CRITIC SMACKDOWN: WINNING THE FIGHT AGAINST NEGATIVE THOUGHTS

That voice in your head that loves telling you that you suck, mess everything up, and should just give up? Yeah, it's the WORST! But guess what? You don't have to listen to that negativity anymore.

This chapter is your ultimate guide to fighting back against your inner critic. We'll cover how to spot those sneaky self-sabotaging thoughts, disarm them with a dose of humor, and replace them with the kind of self-talk a true friend would use. Consider this your training to become a master at shutting down that inner bully and start believing in yourself!

# SPOT THE CRITIC: RECOGNIZING THOSE NEGATIVE SELF-TALK PATTERNS

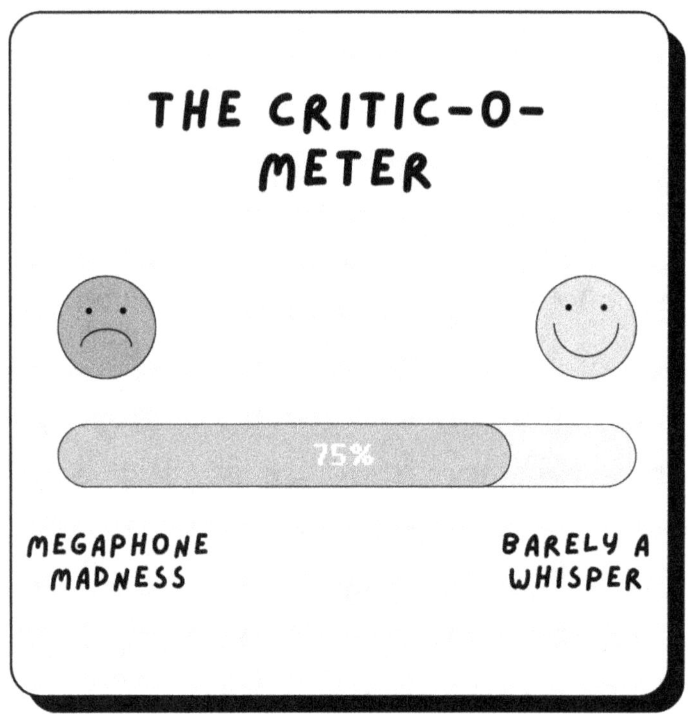


Okay, let's get real. We all have that voice in our heads — the one that's always ready with a put-down predicts epic fails, or whispers that you'll never be as cool/smart/funny as everyone else. It's your inner critic, and if you have anxiety, that voice is basically blasting through a megaphone.

Think of your inner critic like that frenemy who loves to point out everything you did wrong after the fact. The more you listen, the worse you feel. But here's the thing: that voice isn't telling you the truth, even if it seems that way. It's a broken record of negativity, making you doubt yourself at every turn.

The first step to dealing with your inner critic is to get good at spotting it. Start paying attention to that running commentary in your head. What does it say? When does it get extra chatty? Is it all about your looks, your grades, or the fear of saying something embarrassing? Is it worse before a test or when you're heading to a party?

Here's a trick: try to actually picture your critic. Is it a grumpy troll, a judgemental shadow, or maybe a panicked little gremlin? Seeing those negative thoughts as something separate from yourself can help you take them less seriously.

Once you can recognize those critical thoughts, it's time to fight back. Don't just accept everything your inner critic tells you as fact. Start questioning it:

- "I'm gonna bomb this presentation and everyone will think I'm an idiot."
  - **Reframe:** "I practiced, I'm prepared. It might not be perfect, but I'm gonna do my best."
- "If I try to join that conversation, I'll just sound stupid."
  - **Reframe:** "My thoughts are worth sharing, even if I'm nervous."

- "I'm so awkward compared to them."
  - **Reframe:** "I've got my own style, and I'm way more interesting than I give myself credit for."

Challenging your inner critic gets easier with practice. It's like building muscle – the more you do it, the stronger you get. Some days it'll be harder, and that's okay. Just keep noticing those unhelpful thoughts and gently steering yourself towards a kinder, more realistic view.

Think you know your inner critic pretty well? Hold on, because we're about to make it lose all its power by giving it the silliest name imaginable. Think 'Sir Whines-a-lot' or 'Ms. Doom-and-Gloom'. Get ready for some serious laughs!

## PARENT TIP: MODEL MANAGING NEGATIVITY 

- ✓ Narrate Your Struggles: Age-appropriately, share a time you messed up or felt self-doubt: "Ugh, I burned dinner again. Guess I'm not a great cook..." This lets them know everyone has that voice.

- ✓ Show Your Coping Skills: Talk them through how you handle your negativity: "Okay, deep breath. One bad meal doesn't mean I suck, let's order pizza!". Modeling those 'in-the-moment' skills is powerful.

✓ **Self-Compassion Out Loud:** When you slip up, verbalize being kind to yourself: "That wasn't my best parenting moment. Kids mess up, parents do too. I can try again tomorrow."

## IN ACTION: EMILY'S MATH TEST STRUGGLE 

The night before her math test, Emily's anxiety spirals. Her inner critic relentlessly tells her she's doomed to fail and is the worst in the class. Recognizing this familiar negativity, Emily visualizes her critic as a grumpy math troll. Instead of accepting the troll's harsh words, she reframes her perspective. She reminds herself she may not get the best grade, but she does know the basics and will focus on what she's learned. During the test, she still faces difficult questions but manages her anxiety better, allowing her to focus on what she does know. Emily ends up getting a C, proving her inner critic's prediction of total failure was wrong.

# NAME YOUR CRITIC: GIVING YOUR INNER JERK A SILLY NAME MAKES IT LESS POWERFUL

Okay, in the previous section, we learned how to catch your inner critic in the act. Now, we're gonna turn those mean thoughts into a total joke! Get ready to give your inner critic the most embarrassing name imaginable.

Why does this work? Picture a superhero movie – the villain is way less intimidating when they have a dumb name like "The Tickle Monster" instead of some scary, mysterious title. The same goes for your inner critic! Giving it a goofy name helps you see those thoughts as less powerful.

Imagine your inner critic as that annoying kid in class always trying to bring you down. By giving it a name, you're calling it out! Suddenly, instead of a vague, looming dread, it's just "Miss Negative Nancy" or "Panic-Attack Pete" spouting nonsense. Way less scary, right?

The sillier the name, the better! Here's some inspiration:

- Miss Doom-and-Gloom
- Captain Overthinker
- The Whine Machine
- Sir Self-Doubt
- Queen of Catastrophe

Feeling creative? Draw a picture of your inner critic based on its name! A grumpy blob with a frown? A frantic squirrel with its tail on fire? This makes it even funnier.

Next time you hear that familiar put-down ("You'll totally bomb this", "They're just laughing at you", etc.), instead of getting down on yourself, think, "Oh hey, it's Panic-Attack Pete again". Just naming it takes away some of its power.

**Bonus:** Talk back to your critic using its silly name:

- "Chill out, Captain Overthinker, I got this!"
- "Not today, Miss Doom-and-Gloom, I'm trying new things!"

Remember, this takes practice! Your inner critic won't disappear overnight. But the more you do this, the easier it gets to see those thoughts for what they are – a bunch of BS trying to hold you back. Each time you make your critic look like a clown, YOU become stronger.

Think your inner critic is starting to sweat? Good! Next up, we're learning how to politely tell those unhelpful thoughts to buzz off. Get ready for some serious self-confidence boosting!

## IN ACTION: EMILY'S SOCIAL VICTORY

Emily loves hanging out with her close friends, but larger gatherings trigger her inner critic, "Ms. Awkward". Her fears whisper that she'll say something stupid, everyone will stare, and she'll end up hiding in a bathroom all night. Instead of letting those thoughts overwhelm her, Emily starts to picture Ms. Awkward as a jittery cartoon character with huge eyes and a shaky voice. This helps her see the fear as a bit ridiculous. When invited to a party with people she doesn't know well, Emily feels tempted to bail, but she decides to face Ms. Awkward head-on, reminding herself "I can feel nervous and still go!". The first hour of the party is tough, and she does feel a bit out of place, but she finds a friendly face to chat with, which boosts her confidence. Later, she even cracks a joke in a group! While not a perfect night, Emily leaves feeling proud she didn't let her inner critic win.

## EXERCISE 23: CRITIC PROFILE WORKSHEET

✓ Challenge: Understanding your inner critic is the first step to taming it! Fill out this profile to get a better idea of how that negative voice operates. Furthermore, draw a picture of your inner critic below! Seeing it as a cartoon monster or a grumpy old figure can make it seem less intimidating. Here are the steps:

- Name Your Critic: Does it have a specific name? (Ms. Doom-and-Gloom, The Worrywart, etc.) A silly name can take away some of its power.
- The Voice: How does your critic sound? Check all that apply:
  - Grumpy
  - Whiny
  - Sarcastic/Mean
  - Panicked
  - Bossy
  - Other: _______________

- **Target Zones:** What does your inner critic usually attack? Circle your top three:
  - Looks/Body
  - Intelligence/School
  - Social Skills/Friends
  - Personality (being boring, weird, etc.)
  - Sports/Talents
  - Other: _______________
- **Trigger Time:** When is your critic most likely to show up?
  - Before tests/performances
  - In social situations/parties
  - Trying new things
  - When I compare myself to others
  - When I make a mistake
  - Other: _______________
- **Favorite Lines:** What are some typical phrases your inner critic uses? (Examples: "You're so stupid," "You'll never have real friends," "Why even bother?")

# THANK AND DISMISS: HOW TO ACKNOWLEDGE THOSE MEAN THOUGHTS WITHOUT LETTING THEM TAKE OVER

Okay, you've turned your inner critic into a hilarious cartoon villain. Awesome start! But let's face it – "Sir Stress-a-Lot" or "Miss Meltdown" aren't going to vanish just like that. So, what do you do when those pesky thoughts try to rain on your parade? That's where "Thank and Dismiss" comes in.

Imagine someone won't stop yapping in your ear when you're trying to get stuff done. You don't want to be mean, but you also can't take their negativity 24/7. "Thank and Dismiss" is about acknowledging your inner critic, then firmly but politely putting it back in its place. Here's the Play-by-Play:

1. **Spot the Thought:** "Ugh, Captain Catastrophe strikes again! Guess I'll bomb this presentation..."
2. **The Fake-Out "Thanks":** "Okay, Captain, heard you loud and clear. Now, back to my prep." (You're not really grateful, but it throws them off their game).
3. **Refocus like a Boss:** Zero in on the present – your notes, a few deep breaths, how your chair actually feels.

Sounds weird, but thanking your inner critic actually messes with its head! Instead of wrestling those negative thoughts (which just makes them stronger), you're calmly showing them who's in charge. Over time, they start to feel less intense.

**Real-Life Action:**
- **About to join that group chat:** "Miss Negative Nancy pipes up... 'They'll ignore you.' Nice try, Nancy, but I'm going for it."
- **Pre-test panic attack:** "Alright, Professor Panic, I hear the failing prediction. Thanks, but I studied, now I'm doing my best."

Heads Up: This might feel awkward at first. But the more you practice, the easier it becomes to tune out those unhelpful thoughts. Think of it like finally getting that annoying song unstuck from your head.

With a little practice, "Thank and Dismiss" becomes your superpower for those moments when your inner critic tries to hijack your day. You've got this!

Okay, facing down your inner critic is a major win! But let's be real, managing anxiety has its ups and downs. Next up, we're going to wrap up with handling those tough days, staying motivated, and why having your support squad is essential.

Anna loves the idea of being artistic, but gets easily discouraged. Her inner critic is a total art snob, telling her that her drawings are childish and she should give up. Anna's learning to fight back with "Thank and Dismiss". Now she responds with, "Okay, Art Snob, thanks for sharing, but I'm gonna try this new technique anyway." This helps her shift her focus away from the harsh judgment and onto the process of creating – experimenting with colors and simply enjoying the feeling of the pencil on the page. While she doesn't create any masterpieces, Anna is surprised to find elements she actually likes in some of her sketches. This unexpected bit of positive feedback gives her the motivation to keep practicing.

## EXERCISE 24: THE CRITIC GETS SILLIER 

Challenge: Your inner critic can be pretty dramatic, making everything seem like a life-or-death crisis. But what if you took away its power by making it completely ridiculous? Taking those scary thoughts to an absurd extreme breaks their hold over you.

It's like your inner critic is a monster, and you just turned it into a fluffy, squeaky chicken — way less intimidating! This exercise is about having fun and loosening the grip of those negative thoughts. The sillier, the better! Here's how:

1. Jot It Down: Write down a few of your inner critic's typical harsh lines. Examples:
   - "Everyone's going to laugh at me."
   - "I'm going to mess this up so badly."
   - "I'm the worst at this."
2. Get Weird: Now, transform those thoughts into something so over-the-top silly, it's impossible to take seriously. Use wacky characters, funny voices, anything goes! Examples:
   - "My presentation will be attacked by an army of grumpy squirrels!"
   - "Professor Doofus predicts my inevitable failure!"
   - "I'm the worst at this...in the entire galaxy!"

Wrap Up:

# THE JOURNEY AHEAD

# INSIDE THIS PART

Okay, you've unlocked some amazing anxiety-fighting superpowers! Now here's the thing: the journey of building confidence and facing fears never really ends. This is where you take those skills and bravely start using them in the real world. It won't always be easy, and that's totally okay!

In this final section, we'll remind you that you have a whole community behind you. You'll find resources to keep learning and growing, plus ways to connect with others who get it. We'll also share tips for the important grown-ups in your life (parents, teachers, etc.) on how to be your best support system. Remember, progress takes time. Celebrate every win, be kind to yourself on the tough days, and never hesitate to ask for help when you need it!

# YOU ARE NOT ALONE: RESOURCES AND WHERE TO FIND YOUR TRIBE

Okay, let's be real: sometimes, even your most awesome anxiety-fighting skills aren't enough. That's not a sign of weakness – that's life! It happens to everyone. The good news is, there's a whole world of support out there if you know where to look. Think of it like this: Even superheroes have a team backing them up, right?

But how do you know when it's time to expand your support squad? Here are a few signs:

- **You're stuck in the spin cycle:** You're trying your best, but those anxious thoughts and feelings won't quit, and it feels impossible to break free.

- **It's affecting your life way too much:** Anxiety is messing with school, friendships, or doing things you enjoy.
- **You just want to talk to someone who gets it:** Sometimes, you need someone who truly understands the struggle, who won't just say "calm down" or tell you to get over it.

So, what kind of backup are we talking about? Here are a few options:

- **Your People:** Is there a trusted adult in your life – a parent, teacher, relative, or coach – who you can be real with? Sometimes just venting to someone understanding can be a huge relief.
- **School Support:** Most schools have counselors or guidance staff. Their job is to help students with all kinds of challenges, including anxiety.
- **Therapists:** These are the anxiety experts! A therapist can teach you even more powerful coping skills, help you untangle those negative thought patterns, and be your support system when things get tough.
- **Support Groups:** Hearing from other teens dealing with similar things can be incredibly powerful. Check your school, community center, or even online.

Asking for help is a brave move, not a weak one. It means you're committed to taking charge of your well-being, and that's seriously awesome. Don't be afraid to reach out – there are people ready to join your team and help you win this thing!

Okay, let's get real: anxiety can feel incredibly isolating. But here's the thing: you are absolutely, definitely not alone. Tons of teens struggle with anxiety – even some of those people who seem super confident on the outside. Knowing where to turn when things feel overwhelming is key. Here are a few ideas to get you started:

- **Trusted Adults:** Maybe it's a parent, teacher, coach, or school counselor. Talking to someone who cares and understands can make a huge difference.
- **Online Support:** There are awesome websites and online communities specifically for teens with anxiety. Find a list of reputable sites at the end of the book.
- **Helplines:** If you're ever in crisis, there are phone and text lines where you can get immediate help. No problem is too small to reach out. Find a list of reputable helplines at the end of the book.
- **Therapy:** If anxiety is seriously interfering with your life, a therapist can be a game-changer.

Building a support system takes time. Look for friends who are accepting, who truly listen, and who make you feel better (not worse!). Join a club, sports team, or online group focused on something you love – shared interests are a great connector.

You don't have to go through this alone. There's a whole crew of people ready to cheer you on, and amazing resources to help you learn to manage anxiety like a boss. Keep taking those small steps to connect with others and seek help when you need it – that's what true strength looks like!

## IN ACTION: TAKING THE FIRST STEP

✓ **The "I Did It" Moment.** Emily had been hiding her anxiety for way too long. The panic attacks, the constant fear of something terrible happening...it felt like this crushing weight she carried everywhere. Her mom always asked if she was okay, but Emily would just brush it off. Opening up felt terrifying — what if her mom thought she was crazy or overreacting? But one day, she just couldn't take it anymore. After a particularly rough meltdown, she blurted it all out. Turns out, her mom had some anxiety struggles of her own when she was younger. Instead of judgment, Emily got a hug and a promise that they'd figure this out together. For the first time in a long time, Emily felt a tiny flicker of hope instead of that familiar dread.

✓ **Finding the Right Fit.** Michael knew he needed help, but the first few therapists he saw just didn't get it. One gave him advice that felt totally out of touch. Another just kind of nodded along, which wasn't helpful at all. He was starting to feel discouraged, like maybe no one could help him. Then, a friend recommended a therapist who specializes in teens. This one was different. She asked the right questions, challenged him to look at things in a new way, and even had a bit of humor mixed in. Finally, Michael felt like he wasn't just talking at a wall. It wasn't always easy, but it was the first time he felt like therapy might actually work.

## EXERCISE 25: MY SUPPORT CREW BRAINSTORM 

✓ **Challenge:** Sometimes, we don't realize how much support we already have around us, or who we could turn to if we need a boost. Time to map out your potential support squad! You don't have to tackle anxiety alone. Building your support crew takes time, but even knowing those people are out there can make a huge difference!

✓ **Step 1: The Brainstorm.** In a dedicated space below start listing everyone who might have your back, even if you've never actually asked them for help with your anxiety before. Think about:

- **Family:** Parents, siblings, cousins, aunts, uncles, the cool grandparent... anyone!
- **Friends:** Besties, school friends, teammates, even that kid in class who always makes you laugh.
- **Teachers, Coaches, Mentors:** Who do you trust and respect?
- **Online Communities:** Are there safe online groups or forums where you connect with other teens?
- **Professionals:** School counselors, therapists (if you're already seeing one, or might be open to it).

✓ **Step 2: What's Their Superpower?** Next to each person's name, jot down what kind of support they might offer. Here are some ideas:

- **The Listener:** Just need to vent to someone who gets it?
- **The Advice-Giver:** Need practical tips or another perspective?
- **The Distraction Pro:** Helps you take your mind off things when it's all too much.
- **The Cheerleader:** Reminds you of your strengths when you're feeling down.
- **The Practical Helper:** Might run errands with you if places feel overwhelming, or study with you if anxiety makes it hard to focus.

✓ **Step 3: Reflect**

- Were you surprised by anyone on your list?
- Is there a type of support you're lacking?
- Could you reach out to someone this week, even just to start a casual conversation?

# A NOTE FOR PARENTS, TEACHERS, & OTHER CARING ADULTS

Seeing a teen you care about struggle with anxiety can be heartbreaking. You want to fix everything, to take away their pain, but sometimes it feels like you're just saying the wrong things. The good news is, your support can make a world of difference!

It's easy to think, "If they just tried a little harder, they could get through this." But anxiety isn't about willpower or weakness. Their brains are wired to see more danger in the world, making things that seem manageable to others feel overwhelming. Telling them to "calm down" or "get over it" can be as hurtful as telling someone with a broken leg to just "walk it off".

The best thing you can do is be a safe haven. Listen without judgment and let them know you understand how hard this is. Even if their fears seem irrational, they feel very real and scary to the teen experiencing them. Saying things like, "That sounds really tough" or "It makes sense that makes you anxious" can be incredibly powerful.

Remember, anxiety isn't something they can just turn off, but they can learn to manage it. Support them as they try the techniques in this book, and be patient as they build their coping skills. Each small victory, each time they face a fear, is a huge win! Celebrate those moments of bravery. This builds the confidence they need to keep challenging themselves and prove their anxiety doesn't have to define them.

If anxiety starts significantly impacting their life – causing sleep problems, missing school, or constant worry – it's time to seek professional help. A therapist can provide personalized support and teach even more ways to cope.

Supporting an anxious teen can be emotionally draining. Remember to be kind to yourself too. Make time for your own well-being, so you can be the best possible support for them. The teen years are challenging for everyone, especially with anxiety. But with your understanding, encouragement, and the tools they're learning, they absolutely can build the resilience to not just cope, but thrive.

## EXERCISE 26: MY ANXIETY CYCLE

✓ Purpose: To help both parent and teen better understand how anxiety works, creating a shared language for discussing difficult moments.

✓ Instructions:

1. Brainstorm: Start by asking your teen to describe what anxiety feels like in their body (tight chest, racing thoughts, etc.) and what thoughts or worries usually accompany it. Write these down.

2. Draw the Cycle: Draw a large circle (or use the one provided below). Explain that anxiety often works in a cycle, where thoughts, feelings, and physical sensations feed into each other.

3. Fill It In: Place some of the thoughts and feelings your teen mentioned inside the circle. Then, discuss common behaviors that might result from the anxiety (avoiding situations, seeking reassurance, etc.). Write these outside the circle.

4. Find the Triggers: Ask your teen what situations or events tend to set off this cycle. Are there specific places, people, or thoughts that seem to be the starting point? Add a few of these triggers outside the cycle, drawing arrows towards it to show the connection.

5. Identify Coping Tools: Together, brainstorm a few techniques from this book that your teen has found helpful, especially ones that address different points in the cycle. Write these near the cycle.

✓ How to Introduce It:

- Pick the Right Time: Don't do this when your teen is already overwhelmed or having a major anxiety attack. Choose a calm moment when things are going relatively well.

- Be Collaborative: Emphasize that this is about working together to understand their anxiety better, not about you telling them what to do.

- Keep it Simple: The diagram doesn't have to be complex or perfectly organized. The act of mapping it out together is the most important part.

# RESOURCES



- Organizations focused on teen anxiety:
  - https://adaa.org/
  - https://www.nimh.nih.gov/
  - https://childmind.org/
- Websites with teen-friendly articles and self-help tips:
  - https://jedfoundation.org/
  - https://www.mhinnovation.net/organisations/teenmentalhealthorg
  - https://www.youngminds.org.uk/
- Specific resources for CBT or mindfulness:
  - https://www.abct.org/
  - https://www.mindful.org/

BOOKS

- Other teen-focused anxiety guides:
  - "The Shyness and Social Anxiety Workbook for Teens" by Jennifer Shannon
  - "Don't Let Your Emotions Run Your Life for Teens" by Sheri Van Dijk
- CBT workbooks for a broader audience:
  - "Mind Over Mood" by Dennis Greenberger & Christine A. Padesky
  - "The Anxiety and Worry Workbook" by David Carbonell
- Mindfulness books aimed at teens:
  - "Breathe" by Inna Segal
  - "The Mindful Teen" by Dzung Vo

- Mindfulness/Meditation:
  - Headspace
  - Calm
  - Smiling Mind
- CBT-Based Apps:
  - MindShift CBT
  - Wysa
- Mood Tracking:
  - Daylio
  - Moodpath

# IMAGE REFERENCES

Marina Zlochin, Colorful Retro What's Your Current Mood Instagram Post, Canva.com

Canva Creative Studio, Battery, Canva.com

Magrhib, Button Quote Instagram Post, Canva.com

Ayasumak, Simple Line Process Diagram, Canva.com

Deemakdaksina, These Habits Could Harm Your Brain Flyer, Canva.com

Magrhib, Button Quote Instagram Post, Canva.com

Ayasumak, Simple Line Process Diagram, Canva.com

Deemakdaksina, These Habits Could Harm Your Brain Flyer, Canva.com

Garis Studio, Human Body Process Diagram Infographic Graph, Canva.com

Leonora, Iceberg Illusion of Success Infographic Graph, Canva.com

Canva Creative Studio, White Dots Background with Purple Monster, Canva.com

Justice Project, Purple, and Blue Illustrative Cheerleader Quotes Bookmark, Canva.com

Sparrowandsnow, Colorful Illustration Emoji Advice Bubbles Instagram Post, Canva.com

Ayasumak, Blue Casual Bag Description Facebook Post, Canva.com

RemainLabs, Pastel Retro Computer Happy Meter, Canva.com

Teach Sheat, Blue Yellow Superhero Class Captain Sticker, Canva.com

# EXERCISE INDEX

# ACKNOWLEDGMENTS

This book would not have been possible without the support and guidance of many incredible people. First and foremost, I want to express my deepest gratitude to the teens who bravely shared their experiences with anxiety. Your vulnerability and honesty inspired me every step of the way.

I'm immensely thankful to Dr. Claire Miller, whose expertise in CBT for anxiety was invaluable. Your insights and feedback elevated this work beyond what I could have done alone. To my editor, Mark Ellis, thank you for your sharp eye and wordsmithing skills. You transformed my ideas into something clear and engaging for teens. My wonderful family, especially Michael and Emily, your endless patience and encouragement kept me going, even during those late nights of writing.

And finally, to the countless teens who struggle with anxiety – this book is for you. May it be a source of hope and a toolbox for building a braver, more confident life.

# ABOUT THE AUTHOR

Sarah J. Foster is a therapist and specialist in teen mental health. With over a decade of experience, she's passionate about empowering young people to understand and overcome their struggles. Sarah's own experience with anxiety as a teenager fueled her desire to create a resource she wished she'd had back then. She is also a parenting coach, offering support and guidance to parents navigating the challenges of raising children from toddlers to teens.

Drawing on both her professional expertise and personal journey, Sarah offers practical, down-to-earth guidance in a relatable way. She strongly believes that even the toughest anxiety issues can be managed with the right tools and consistent practice.

When not writing or seeing clients, Sarah can be found hiking with her family, attempting to learn the piano, or experimenting with new vegetarian recipes.

**Also by Sarah J. Foster:**

*Building Bright Minds: A Gentle Parenting Guide for Raising Mentally Strong and Emotionally Healthy Kids*

# Your Child's Journey, Every Step of the Way!

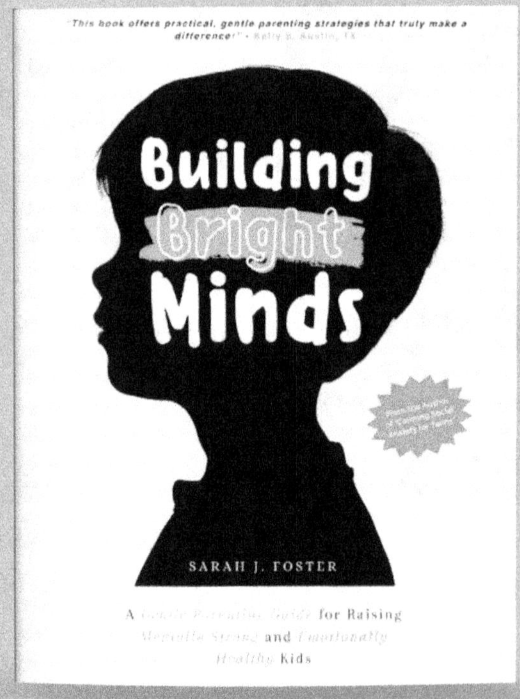


You've equipped your teen with tools in *"Calming Social Anxiety for Teens."* Now, explore *"Building Bright Minds"* by the same author.

**Discover everyday tools to navigate:**
- **Cooperation & Learning**
- **Tantrums & Frustrations**
- **Building a Strong Bond**

**Learn More & Raise Thriving Children of All Ages with *"Building Bright Minds".***